KITÁB-I-ÍQÁN
The Book
of
Certitude

KITÁB-I-ÍQÁN
The Book
of
Certitude

by Bahá'u'lláh

Translated
by
Shoghi Effendi

BAHÁ'Í PUBLISHING TRUST
WILMETTE, ILLINOIS 60091

This translation by Shoghi Effendi was
first published in 1931. A second edition
with an introduction and index was published in 1950 and was subsequently printed
seven times. First pocket-size edition 1983.
Reprinted 1985, 1989

ISBN 0-87743-022-5 hardcover

ISBN 0-87743-189-2 pocket size

Library of Congress Catalog Card No. 51-22838

PRINTED IN THE UNITED STATES OF AMERICA

FOREWORD

This is one more attempt to introduce to the West, in language however inadequate, this book of unsurpassed pre-eminence among the writings of the Author of the Bahá'í Revelation. The hope is that it may assist others in their efforts to approach what must always be regarded as the unattainable goal—a befitting rendering of Bahá'u'lláh's matchless utterance.

SHOGHI

PART ONE

IN THE NAME OF OUR LORD, THE EXALTED, THE MOST HIGH.

NO man shall attain the shores of the ocean of true understanding except he be detached from all that is in heaven and on earth. Sanctify your souls, O ye peoples of the world, that haply ye may attain that station which God hath destined for you and enter thus the tabernacle which, according to the dispensations of Providence, hath been raised in the firmament of the Bayán.

THE essence of these words is this: they that tread the path of faith, they that thirst for the wine of certitude, must cleanse themselves of all that is earthly—their ears from idle talk, their minds from vain imaginings, their hearts from worldly affections, their eyes from that which perisheth. They should put their trust in God, and, holding fast unto Him, follow in His way. Then will they be made worthy of the effulgent glories of the sun of divine knowledge and understanding, and become the recipients of a grace that is infinite and unseen, inasmuch as man can never hope to attain unto the knowledge of the All-Glorious, can never quaff from the stream of divine knowledge and wisdom, can never enter the abode of immortality, nor partake of the cup of divine nearness and favour, unless and until he ceases to regard the words and deeds of mortal men as a standard for the true understanding and recognition of God and His Prophets.

Consider the past. How many, both high and low, have, at all times, yearningly awaited the advent of the Manifestations of God in the sanctified persons of His chosen Ones. How often have they expected His coming, how frequently have they prayed that the breeze of divine mercy might blow, and the promised Beauty step forth from behind the veil of concealment, and be made manifest to all the world. And whensoever the portals of grace did open, and the clouds of divine bounty did rain upon mankind, and the light of the Unseen did shine above the horizon of celestial might, they all denied Him, and turned away from His face—the face of God Himself. Refer ye, to verify this truth, to that which hath been recorded in every sacred Book.

Ponder for a moment, and reflect upon that which hath been the cause of such denial on the part of those who have searched with such earnestness and longing. Their attack hath been more fierce than tongue or pen can describe. Not one single Manifestation of Holiness hath appeared but He was afflicted by the denials, the repudiation, and the vehement opposition of the people around Him. Thus it hath been revealed: "O the misery of men! No Messenger cometh unto them but they laugh Him to scorn."[1] Again He saith: "Each nation hath plotted darkly against their Messenger to lay violent hold on Him, and disputed with vain words to invalidate the truth."[2]

In like manner, those words that have streamed forth from the source of power and descended from the heaven of glory are innumerable and beyond the ordinary comprehension of man. To them that are possessed of true understanding and insight the Súrah of Húd surely sufficeth. Ponder a while those holy words in your heart, and, with utter detachment, strive to grasp their meaning. Examine the wondrous behaviour of the Prophets, and recall the defamations and denials uttered by

[1] Qur'án 36:30.
[2] Qur'án 40:5.

the children of negation and falsehood, perchance you may cause the bird of the human heart to wing its flight away from the abodes of heedlessness and doubt unto the nest of faith and certainty, and drink deep from the pure waters of ancient wisdom, and partake of the fruit of the tree of divine knowledge. Such is the share of the pure in heart of the bread that hath descended from the realms of eternity and holiness.

Should you acquaint yourself with the indignities heaped upon the Prophets of God, and apprehend the true causes of the objections voiced by their oppressors, you will surely appreciate the significance of their position. Moreover, the more closely you observe the denials of those who have opposed the Manifestations of the divine attributes, the firmer will be your faith in the Cause of God. Accordingly, a brief mention will be made in this Tablet of divers accounts relative to the Prophets of God, that they may demonstrate the truth that throughout all ages and centuries the Manifestations of power and glory have been subjected to such heinous cruelties that no pen dare describe them. Perchance this may enable a few to cease to be perturbed by the clamour and protestations

of the divines and the foolish of this age, and
cause them to strengthen their confidence and certainty.

Among the Prophets was Noah. For nine hundred and fifty years He prayerfully exhorted His
people and summoned them to the haven of se-
curity and peace. None, however, heeded His call.
Each day they inflicted on His blessed person such
pain and suffering that no one believed He could
survive. How frequently they denied Him, how
malevolently they hinted their suspicion against
Him! Thus it hath been revealed: "And as often
as a company of His people passed by Him, they
derided Him. To them He said: 'Though ye scoff
at us now, we will scoff at you hereafter even as
ye scoff at us. In the end ye shall know.' " [1] Long
afterward, He several times promised victory to
His companions and fixed the hour thereof. But
when the hour struck, the divine promise was not
fulfilled. This caused a few among the small number of His followers to turn away from Him, and
to this testify the records of the best-known books.
These you must certainly have perused; if not, undoubtedly you will. Finally, as stated in books and

[1] Qur'án 11:38.

traditions, there remained with Him only forty or seventy-two of His followers. At last from the depth of His being He cried aloud: "Lord! Leave not upon the land a single dweller from among the unbelievers." [1]

And now, consider and reflect a moment upon the waywardness of this people. What could have been the reason for such denial and avoidance on their part? What could have induced them to refuse to put off the garment of denial, and to adorn themselves with the robe of acceptance? Moreover, what could have caused the nonfulfilment of the divine promise which led the seekers to reject that which they had accepted? Meditate profoundly, that the secret of things unseen may be revealed unto you, that you may inhale the sweetness of a spiritual and imperishable fragrance, and that you may acknowledge the truth that from time immemorial even unto eternity the Almighty hath tried, and will continue to try, His servants, so that light may be distinguished from darkness, truth from falsehood, right from wrong, guidance from error, happiness from misery, and roses from thorns. Even as He hath revealed: "Do men think when

[1] Qur'án 71:26.

they say 'We believe' they shall be let alone and not be put to proof?" [1]

And after Noah the light of the countenance of Húd shone forth above the horizon of creation. For well-nigh seven hundred years, according to the sayings of men, He exhorted the people to turn their faces and draw nearer unto the Riḍván of the divine presence. What showers of afflictions rained upon Him, until at last His adjurations bore the fruit of increased rebelliousness, and His assiduous endeavours resulted in the wilful blindness of His people. "And their unbelief shall only increase for the unbelievers their own perdition." [2]

And after Him there appeared from the Riḍván of the Eternal, the Invisible, the holy person of Ṣáliḥ, Who again summoned the people to the river of everlasting life. For over a hundred years He admonished them to hold fast unto the commandments of God and eschew that which is forbidden. His admonitions, however, yielded no fruit, and His pleading proved of no avail. Several times He retired and lived in seclusion. All this, although that eternal Beauty was summoning

[1] Qur'án 29:2.
[2] Qur'án 35:39.

the people to no other than the city of God. Even as it is revealed: "And unto the tribe of Thamúd We sent their brother Ṣáliḥ. 'O my people,' said He, 'Worship God, ye have none other God beside Him. . . .' They made reply: 'O Ṣáliḥ, our hopes were fixed on thee until now; forbiddest thou us to worship that which our fathers worshipped? Truly we misdoubt that whereunto thou callest us as suspicious.'"[1] All this proved fruitless, until at last there went up a great cry, and all fell into utter perdition.

Later, the beauty of the countenance of the Friend of God[2] appeared from behind the veil, and another standard of divine guidance was hoisted. He invited the people of the earth to the light of righteousness. The more passionately He exhorted them, the fiercer waxed the envy and waywardness of the people, except those who wholly detached themselves from all save God, and ascended on the wings of certainty to the station which God hath exalted beyond the comprehension of men. It is well known what a host of enemies besieged Him, until at last the fires of envy and rebellion were kindled against Him.

[1] Qur'án 11:61, 62.
[2] Abraham.

And after the episode of the fire came to pass, He, the lamp of God amongst men, was, as recorded in all books and chronicles, expelled from His city.

And when His day was ended, there came the turn of Moses. Armed with the rod of celestial dominion, adorned with the white hand of divine knowledge, and proceeding from the Párán of the love of God, and wielding the serpent of power and everlasting majesty, He shone forth from the Sinai of light upon the world. He summoned all the peoples and kindreds of the earth to the kingdom of eternity, and invited them to partake of the fruit of the tree of faithfulness. Surely you are aware of the fierce opposition of Pharaoh and his people, and of the stones of idle fancy which the hands of infidels cast upon that blessed Tree. So much so that Pharaoh and his people finally arose and exerted their utmost endeavour to extinguish with the waters of falsehood and denial the fire of that sacred Tree, oblivious of the truth that no earthly water can quench the flame of divine wisdom, nor mortal blasts extinguish the lamp of everlasting dominion. Nay, rather, such water cannot but intensify the burning of the flame, and such

[11]

blasts cannot but ensure the preservation of the lamp, were ye to observe with the eye of discernment, and walk in the way of God's holy will and pleasure. How well hath a believer of the kindred of Pharaoh, whose story is recounted by the All-Glorious in His Book revealed unto His beloved One, observed: "And a man of the family of Pharaoh who was a believer and concealed his faith said: 'Will ye slay a man because he saith my Lord is God, when He hath already come to you with signs from your Lord? If he be a liar, on him will be his lie, but if he be a man of truth, part of what he threateneth will fall upon you. In truth God guideth not him who is a transgressor, a liar.'"[1] Finally, so great was their iniquity that this self-same believer was put to a shameful death. "The curse of God be upon the people of tyranny."[2]

And now, ponder upon these things. What could have caused such contention and conflict? Why is it that the advent of every true Manifestation of God hath been accompanied by such strife and tumult, by such tyranny and upheaval? This notwithstanding the fact that all the Prophets of God,

[1] Qur'án 40:28.   [2] Qur'án 11:21.

whenever made manifest unto the peoples of the world, have invariably foretold the coming of yet another Prophet after them, and have established such signs as would herald the advent of the future Dispensation. To this the records of all sacred books bear witness. Why then is it that despite the expectation of men in their quest of the Manifestations of Holiness, and in spite of the signs recorded in the sacred books, such acts of violence, of oppression and cruelty, should have been perpetrated in every age and cycle against all the Prophets and chosen Ones of God? Even as He hath revealed: "As oft as an Apostle cometh unto you with that which your souls desire not, ye swell with pride, accusing some of being impostors and slaying others." [1]

Reflect, what could have been the motive for such deeds? What could have prompted such behaviour towards the Revealers of the beauty of the All-Glorious? Whatever in days gone by hath been the cause of the denial and opposition of those people hath now led to the perversity of the people of this age. To maintain that the testimony of Providence was incomplete, that it hath therefore

[1] Qur'án 2:87.

been the cause of the denial of the people, is but open blasphemy. How far from the grace of the All-Bountiful and from His loving providence and tender mercies it is to single out a soul from amongst all men for the guidance of His creatures, and, on one hand, to withhold from Him the full measure of His divine testimony, and, on the other, inflict severe retribution on His people for having turned away from His chosen One! Nay, the manifold bounties of the Lord of all beings have, at all times, through the Manifestations of His divine Essence, encompassed the earth and all that dwell therein. Not for a moment hath His grace been withheld, nor have the showers of His loving-kindness ceased to rain upon mankind. Consequently, such behaviour can be attributed to naught save the petty-mindedness of such souls as tread the valley of arrogance and pride, are lost in the wilds of remoteness, walk in the ways of their idle fancy, and follow the dictates of the leaders of their faith. Their chief concern is mere opposition; their sole desire is to ignore the truth. Unto every discerning observer it is evident and manifest that had these people in the days of each of the Manifestations of the Sun of Truth sanctified their eyes, their ears, and their hearts from whatever they had seen, heard, and felt, they surely would not have been deprived of beholding the beauty of God, nor strayed far from the habitations of glory. But having weighed the testimony of God by the standard of their own knowledge, gleaned from the teachings of the leaders of their faith, and found it at variance with their limited understanding, they arose to perpetrate such unseemly acts.

Leaders of religion, in every age, have hindered their people from attaining the shores of eternal salvation, inasmuch as they held the reins of authority in their mighty grasp. Some for the lust of leadership, others through want of knowledge and understanding, have been the cause of the deprivation of the people. By their sanction and authority, every Prophet of God hath drunk from the chalice of sacrifice, and winged His flight unto the heights of glory. What unspeakable cruelties they that have occupied the seats of authority and learning have inflicted upon the true Monarchs of the world, those Gems of divine virtue! Content with a transitory dominion, they have deprived themselves of an everlasting sovereignty. Thus, their eyes beheld not the light of the countenance of the Well-Beloved, nor did their ears hearken unto the sweet melodies of the Bird of Desire. For this reason, in all sacred books mention hath been made of the divines of every age. Thus He saith: "O people of the Book! Why disbelieve the signs of God to which ye yourselves have been witnesses?"[1] And also He saith: "O people of the Book! Why clothe ye the truth with falsehood? Why wittingly hide the truth?"[2] Again, He saith: "Say, O people of the Book! Why repel believers from the way of God?"[3] It is evident that by the "people of the Book," who have repelled their fellow-men from the straight path of God, is meant none other than the divines of that age, whose names and character have been revealed in the sacred books, and alluded to in the verses and traditions recorded therein, were you to observe with the eye of God.

With fixed and steady gaze, born of the unerring eye of God, scan for a while the horizon of divine knowledge, and contemplate those words of perfection which the Eternal hath revealed, that haply the mysteries of divine wisdom, hidden ere now beneath the veil of glory and treasured within the tabernacle of His grace, may be made manifest

[1] Qur'án 3:70.
[2] Qur'án 3:71.
[3] Qur'án 3:99.

unto you. The denials and protestations of these leaders of religion have, in the main, been due to their lack of knowledge and understanding. Those words uttered by the Revealers of the beauty of the one true God, setting forth the signs that should herald the advent of the Manifestation to come, they never understood nor fathomed. Hence they raised the standard of revolt, and stirred up mischief and sedition. It is obvious and manifest that the true meaning of the utterances of the Birds of Eternity is revealed to none except those that manifest the Eternal Being, and the melodies of the Nightingale of Holiness can reach no ear save that of the denizens of the everlasting realm. The Copt of tyranny can never partake of the cup touched by the lips of the Sept of justice, and the Pharaoh of unbelief can never hope to recognize the hand of the Moses of truth. Even as He saith: "None knoweth the meaning thereof except God and them that are well-grounded in knowledge."[1] And yet, they have sought the interpretation of the Book from those that are wrapt in veils, and have refused to seek enlightenment from the fountainhead of knowledge.

And when the days of Moses were ended, and

[1] Qur'án 3:7.

the light of Jesus, shining forth from the day-spring of the Spirit, encompassed the world, all the people of Israel arose in protest against Him. They clamoured that He Whose advent the Bible had foretold must needs promulgate and fulfil the laws of Moses, whereas this youthful Nazarene, who laid claim to the station of the divine Messiah, had annulled the law of divorce and of the sabbath day—the most weighty of all the laws of Moses. Moreover, what of the signs of the Manifestation yet to come? These people of Israel are even unto the present day still expecting that Manifestation which the Bible hath foretold! How many Manifestations of Holiness, how many Revealers of the light everlasting, have appeared since the time of Moses, and yet Israel, wrapt in the densest veils of satanic fancy and false imaginings, is still expectant that the idol of her own handiwork will appear with such signs as she herself hath conceived! Thus hath God laid hold of them for their sins, hath extinguished in them the spirit of faith, and tormented them with the flames of the nethermost fire. And this for no other reason except that Israel refused to apprehend the meaning of such words as have been revealed in the Bible concerning the signs of the coming Revelation. As she never grasped their true significance, and, to outward seeming, such events never came to pass, she, therefore, remained deprived of recognizing the beauty of Jesus and of beholding the face of God. And they still await His coming! From time immemorial even unto this day, all the kindreds and peoples of the earth have clung to such fanciful and unseemly thoughts, and thus have deprived themselves of the clear waters streaming from the springs of purity and holiness.

In unfolding these mysteries, We have, in Our former Tablets which were addressed to a friend in the melodious language of Ḥijáz, cited a few of the verses revealed unto the Prophets of old. And now, responding to your request, We again shall cite, in these pages, those same verses, uttered this time in the wondrous accents of 'Iráq, that haply the sore athirst in the wilds of remoteness may attain unto the ocean of the divine presence, and they that languish in the wastes of separation be led unto the home of eternal reunion. Thus the mists of error may be dispelled, and the all-resplendent light of divine guidance dawn forth above the horizon of human hearts. In God We put Our trust, and to Him We cry for help, that haply there may flow from this pen that which shall quicken the souls of men, that they may all arise from their beds of heedlessness and hearken unto the rustling of the leaves of Paradise, from the tree which the hand of divine power hath, by the permission of God, planted in the Riḍván of the All-Glorious.

To them that are endowed with understanding, it is clear and manifest that when the fire of the love of Jesus consumed the veils of Jewish limitations, and His authority was made apparent and partially enforced, He the Revealer of the unseen Beauty, addressing one day His disciples, referred unto His passing, and, kindling in their hearts the fire of bereavement, said unto them: "I go away and come again unto you." And in another place He said: "I go and another will come Who will tell you all that I have not told you, and will fulfil all that I have said." Both these sayings have but one meaning, were you to ponder upon the Manifestations of the Unity of God with divine insight.

Every discerning observer will recognize that in the Dispensation of the Qur'án both the Book and the Cause of Jesus were confirmed. As to the matter of names, Muḥammad, Himself, declared: "I am Jesus." He recognized the truth of the signs, prophecies, and words of Jesus, and testified that they were all of God. In this sense, neither the person of Jesus nor His writings hath differed from that of Muḥammad and of His holy Book, inasmuch as both have championed the Cause of God, uttered His praise, and revealed His commandments. Thus it is that Jesus, Himself, declared: "I go away and come again unto you." Consider the sun. Were it to say now, "I am the sun of yesterday," it would speak the truth. And should it, bearing the sequence of time in mind, claim to be other than that sun, it still would speak the truth. In like manner, if it be said that all the days are but one and the same, it is correct and true. And if it be said, with respect to their particular names and designations, that they differ, that again is true. For though they are the same, yet one doth recognize in each a separate designation, a specific attribute, a particular character. Conceive accordingly the distinction, variation, and unity characteristic of the various Manifestations of holiness, that thou mayest comprehend the allusions made by the creator of all names and attributes to the mysteries of distinction and unity, and discover the answer to thy question as to why that everlasting Beauty should have, at sundry times, called Himself by different names and titles.

Afterwards, the companions and disciples of Jesus asked Him concerning those signs that must needs signalize the return of His manifestation. When, they asked, shall these things be? Several times they questioned that peerless Beauty, and, every time He made reply, He set forth a special sign that should herald the advent of the promised Dispensation. To this testify the records of the four Gospels.

This wronged One will cite but one of these instances, thus conferring upon mankind, for the sake of God, such bounties as are yet concealed within the treasury of the hidden and sacred Tree, that haply mortal men may not remain deprived of their share of the immortal fruit, and attain to a dewdrop of the waters of everlasting life which, from Baghdád, the "Abode of Peace," are being vouchsafed unto all mankind. We ask for neither meed nor reward. "We nourish your souls for the sake of God; we seek from you neither recompense nor thanks." [1] This is the food that conferreth ever-

[1] Qur'án 76:9.

lasting life upon the pure in heart and the illumined in spirit. This is the bread of which it is said: "Lord, send down upon us Thy bread from heaven." [1] This bread shall never be withheld from them that deserve it, nor can it ever be exhausted. It groweth everlastingly from the tree of grace; it descendeth at all seasons from the heavens of justice and mercy. Even as He saith: "Seest thou not to what God likeneth a good word? To a good tree; its root firmly fixed, and its branches reaching unto heaven: yielding its fruit in all seasons." [2]

O the pity! that man should deprive himself of this goodly gift, this imperishable bounty, this everlasting life. It behooveth him to prize this food that cometh from heaven, that perchance, through the wondrous favours of the Sun of Truth, the dead may be brought to life, and withered souls be quickened by the infinite Spirit. Make haste, O my brother, that while there is yet time our lips may taste of the immortal draught, for the breeze of life, now blowing from the city of the Well-Beloved, cannot last, and the streaming river of holy utterance must needs be stilled, and the portals of the Riḍván cannot for ever remain open. The day

[1] Qur'án 5:117.
[2] Qur'án 14:24.

will surely come when the Nightingale of Paradise will have winged its flight away from its earthly abode unto its heavenly nest. Then will its melody be heard no more, and the beauty of the rose cease to shine. Seize the time, therefore, ere the glory of the divine springtime hath spent itself, and the Bird of Eternity ceased to warble its melody, that thy inner hearing may not be deprived of hearkening unto its call. This is My counsel unto thee and unto the beloved of God. Whosoever wisheth, let him turn thereunto; whosoever wisheth, let him turn away. God, verily, is independent of him and of that which he may see and witness.

These are the melodies, sung by Jesus, Son of Mary, in accents of majestic power in the Riḍván of the Gospel, revealing those signs that must needs herald the advent of the Manifestation after Him. In the first Gospel according to Matthew it is recorded: And when they asked Jesus concerning the signs of His coming, He said unto them: "Immediately after the oppression [1] of those days shall the sun be darkened, and the moon shall not give her light, and the stars shall fall from heaven, and the powers of the earth shall be shaken: and then

[1] The Greek word used (Thlipsis) has two meanings: pressure and oppression.

shall appear the sign of the Son of man in heaven:
and then shall all the tribes of the earth mourn,
and they shall see the Son of man coming in the
clouds of heaven with power and great glory. And
he shall send his angels with a great sound of a
trumpet." [1] Rendered into the Persian tongue,[2] the
purport of these words is as follows: When the
oppression and afflictions that are to befall mankind will have come to pass, then shall the sun
be withheld from shining, the moon from giving
light, the stars of heaven shall fall upon the earth,
and the pillars of the earth shall quake. At that
time, the signs of the Son of man shall appear in
heaven, that is, the promised Beauty and Substance
of life shall, when these signs have appeared, step
forth out of the realm of the invisible into the visible world. And He saith: at that time, all the
peoples and kindreds that dwell on earth shall bewail and lament, and they shall see that divine
Beauty coming from heaven, riding upon the
clouds with power, grandeur, and magnificence,
sending His angels with a great sound of a trumpet. Similarly, in the three other Gospels, according to Luke, Mark, and John, the same statements

[1] Matthew 24:29-31.
[2] The passage is quoted by Bahá'u'lláh in Arabic and interpreted in Persian.

are recorded. As We have referred at length to these in Our Tablets revealed in the Arabic tongue, We have made no mention of them in these pages, and have confined Ourselves to but one reference.

Inasmuch as the Christian divines have failed to apprehend the meaning of these words, and did not recognize their object and purpose, and have clung to the literal interpretation of the words of Jesus, they therefore became deprived of the streaming grace of the Muḥammadan Revelation and its showering bounties. The ignorant among the Christian community, following the example of the leaders of their faith, were likewise prevented from beholding the beauty of the King of glory, inasmuch as those signs which were to accompany the dawn of the sun of the Muḥammadan Dispensation did not actually come to pass. Thus, ages have passed and centuries rolled away, and that most pure Spirit hath repaired unto the retreats of its ancient sovereignty. Once more hath the eternal Spirit breathed into the mystic trumpet, and caused the dead to speed out of their sepulchres of heedlessness and error unto the realm of guidance and grace. And yet, that expectant community still crieth out: When shall these things be? When shall the promised One, the object of our expectation, be made manifest, that we may arise for the triumph of His Cause, that we may sacrifice our substance for His sake, that we may offer up our lives in His path? In like manner, have such false imaginings caused other communities to stray from the Kawthar of the infinite mercy of Providence, and to be busied with their own idle thoughts.

Beside this passage, there is yet another verse in the Gospel wherein He saith: "Heaven and earth shall pass away: but My words shall not pass away." [1] Thus it is that the adherents of Jesus maintained that the law of the Gospel shall never be annulled, and that whensoever the promised Beauty is made manifest and all the signs are revealed, He must needs re-affirm and establish the law proclaimed in the Gospel, so that there may remain in the world no faith but His faith. This is their fundamental belief. And their conviction is such that were a person to be made manifest with all the promised signs and to promulgate that which is contrary to the letter of the law of the Gos-

[1] Luke 21 :33.

pel, they must assuredly renounce him, refuse to submit to his law, declare him an infidel, and laugh him to scorn. This is proved by that which came to pass when the sun of the Muḥammadan Revelation was revealed. Had they sought with a humble mind from the Manifestations of God in every Dispensation the true meaning of these words revealed in the sacred books—words the misapprehension of which hath caused men to be deprived of the recognition of the Sadratu'l-Muntahá, the ultimate Purpose—they surely would have been guided to the light of the Sun of Truth, and would have discovered the mysteries of divine knowledge and wisdom.

This servant will now share with thee a dewdrop out of the fathomless ocean of the truths treasured in these holy words, that haply discerning hearts may comprehend all the allusions and the implications of the utterances of the Manifestations of Holiness, so that the overpowering majesty of the Word of God may not prevent them from attaining unto the ocean of His names and attributes, nor deprive them of recognizing the Lamp of God which is the seat of the revelation of His glorified Essence.

As to the words—"Immediately after the oppression of those days"—they refer to the time when men shall become oppressed and afflicted, the time when the lingering traces of the Sun of Truth and the fruit of the Tree of knowledge and wisdom will have vanished from the midst of men, when the reins of mankind will have fallen into the grasp of the foolish and ignorant, when the portals of divine unity and understanding—the essential and highest purpose in creation—will have been closed, when certain knowledge will have given way to idle fancy, and corruption will have usurped the station of righteousness. Such a condition as this is witnessed in this day when the reins of every community have fallen into the grasp of foolish leaders, who lead after their own whims and desire. On their tongue the mention of God hath become an empty name; in their midst His holy Word a dead letter. Such is the sway of their desires, that the lamp of conscience and reason hath been quenched in their hearts, and this although the fingers of divine power have unlocked the portals of the knowledge of God, and the light of divine knowledge and heavenly grace hath illumined and inspired the essence of all created things, in such wise that in each and every thing a door of knowledge hath been opened, and within every atom traces of the sun hath been made manifest. And yet, in spite of all these manifold revelations of divine knowledge, which have encompassed the world, they still vainly imagine the door of knowledge to be closed, and the showers of mercy to be stilled. Clinging unto idle fancy, they have strayed far from the 'Urvatu'l-Vuthqá of divine knowledge. Their hearts seem not to be inclined to knowledge and the door thereof, neither think they of its manifestations, inasmuch as in idle fancy they have found the door that leadeth unto earthly riches, whereas in the manifestation of the Revealer of knowledge they find naught but the call to self-sacrifice. They therefore naturally hold fast unto the former, and flee from the latter. Though they recognize in their hearts the Law of God to be one and the same, yet from every direction they issue a new command, and in every season proclaim a fresh decree. No two are found to agree on one and the same law, for they seek no God but their own desire, and tread no path but the path of error. In leadership they have recognized the ultimate object of their endeavour, and account pride and haughtiness as the highest attainments of their heart's desire. They have placed their sordid machinations above the divine decree, have renounced resignation unto the will of God, busied themselves with selfish calculation, and walked in the way of the hypocrite. With all their power and strength they strive to secure themselves in their petty pursuits, fearful lest the least discredit undermine their authority or blemish the display of their magnificence. Were the eye to be anointed and illumined with the collyrium of the knowledge of God, it would surely discover that a number of voracious beasts have gathered and preyed upon the carrion of the souls of men.

What "oppression" is greater than that which hath been recounted? What "oppression" is more grievous than that a soul seeking the truth, and wishing to attain unto the knowledge of God, should know not where to go for it and from whom to seek it? For opinions have sorely differed, and the ways unto the attainment of God have multiplied. This "oppression" is the essential feature of every Revelation. Unless it cometh to pass, the Sun of Truth will not be made manifest. For the break of the morn of divine guidance must needs follow the darkness of the night of error. For this reason, in all chronicles and traditions reference hath been made unto these things, namely that iniquity shall cover the surface of the earth and darkness shall envelop mankind. As the traditions referred to are well known, and as the purpose of this servant is to be brief, He will refrain from quoting the text of these traditions.

Were this "oppression" (which literally meaneth pressure) to be interpreted that the earth is to become contracted, or were men's idle fancy to conceive similar calamities to befall mankind, it is clear and manifest that no such happenings can ever come to pass. They will assuredly protest that this pre-requisite of divine revelation hath not been made manifest. Such hath been and still is their contention. Whereas, by "oppression" is meant the want of capacity to acquire spiritual knowledge and apprehend the Word of God. By it is meant that when the Day-star of Truth hath set, and the mirrors that reflect His light have departed, mankind will become afflicted with "oppression" and hardship, knowing not whither to turn for guidance. Thus We instruct thee in the interpretation of the traditions, and reveal unto thee the mysteries of divine wisdom, that haply thou mayest comprehend the meaning thereof, and be of them that have quaffed the cup of divine knowledge and understanding.

And now, concerning His words—"The sun shall be darkened, and the moon shall not give light, and the stars shall fall from heaven." By the terms "sun" and "moon," mentioned in the writings of the Prophets of God, is not meant solely the sun and moon of the visible universe. Nay rather, manifold are the meanings they have intended for these terms. In every instance they have attached to them a particular significance. Thus, by the "sun" in one sense is meant those Suns of Truth Who rise from the dayspring of ancient glory, and fill the world with a liberal effusion of grace from on high. These Suns of Truth are the universal Manifestations of God in the worlds of His attributes and names, even as the visible sun that assisteth, as decreed by God, the true One, the Adored, in the development of all earthly things, such as the trees, the fruits, and colours thereof, the minerals of the earth, and all that may be witnessed in the world of creation, so do the divine Luminaries, by their loving care and educative influence, cause the trees of divine unity, the fruits of His oneness, the leaves of detachment, the blossoms of knowledge and certitude, and the myrtles of wisdom and utterance, to exist and be made manifest. Thus it is that through the rise of these Luminaries of God the world is made new, the waters of everlasting life stream forth, the billows of loving-kindness surge, the clouds of grace are gathered, and the breeze of bounty bloweth upon all created things. It is the warmth that these Luminaries of God generate, and the undying fires they kindle, which cause the light of the love of God to burn fiercely in the heart of humanity. It is through the abundant grace of these Symbols of Detachment that the Spirit of life everlasting is breathed into the bodies of the dead. Assuredly the visible sun is but a sign of the splendour of that Day-star of Truth, that Sun Which can never have a peer, a likeness, or rival. Through Him all things live, move, and have their being. Through His grace they are made manifest, and unto Him they all return. From Him all things have sprung, and unto the treasuries of His revelation they all have repaired. From Him all created things did proceed, and to the depositories of His law they did revert.

That these divine Luminaries seem to be confined at times to specific designations and attributes, as you have observed and are now observing, is due solely to the imperfect and limited comprehension of certain minds. Otherwise, they have been at all times, and will through eternity continue to be, exalted above every praising name, and sanctified from every descriptive attribute. The quintessence of every name can hope for no access unto their court of holiness, and the highest and purest of all attributes can never approach their kingdom of glory. Immeasurably high are the Prophets of God exalted above the comprehension of men, who can never know them except by their own Selves. Far be it from His glory that His chosen Ones should be magnified by any other than their own persons. Glorified are they above the praise of men; exalted are they above human understanding!

The term "suns" hath many a time been applied in the writings of the "immaculate Souls" unto the Prophets of God, those luminous Emblems of Detachment. Among those writings are the following words recorded in the "Prayer of Nudbih": [1] "Whither are gone the resplendent Suns? Whereunto have departed those shining Moons and

[1] "Lamentation" attributed to the Twelfth Imám.

sparkling Stars?" Thus, it hath become evident that the terms "sun," "moon," and "stars" primarily signify the Prophets of God, the saints, and their companions, those Luminaries, the light of Whose knowledge hath shed illumination upon the worlds of the visible and the invisible.

In another sense, by these terms is intended the divines of the former Dispensation, who live in the days of the subsequent Revelations, and who hold the reins of religion in their grasp. If these divines be illumined by the light of the latter Revelation they will be acceptable unto God, and will shine with a light everlasting. Otherwise, they will be declared as darkened, even though to outward seeming they be leaders of men, inasmuch as belief and unbelief, guidance and error, felicity and misery, light and darkness, are all dependent upon the sanction of Him Who is the Day-star of Truth. Whosoever among the divines of every age receiveth, in the Day of Reckoning, the testimony of faith from the Source of true knowledge, he verily becometh the recipient of learning, of divine favour, and of the light of true understanding. Otherwise, he is branded as guilty of folly, denial, blasphemy, and oppression.

It is evident and manifest unto every discerning observer that even as the light of the star fadeth before the effulgent splendour of the sun, so doth the luminary of earthly knowledge, of wisdom, and understanding vanish into nothingness when brought face to face with the resplendent glories of the Sun of Truth, the Day-star of divine enlightenment.

That the term "sun" hath been applied to the leaders of religion is due to their lofty position, their fame, and renown. Such are the universally recognized divines of every age, who speak with authority, and whose fame is securely established. If they be in the likeness of the Sun of Truth, they will surely be accounted as the most exalted of all luminaries; otherwise, they are to be recognized as the focal centres of hellish fire. Even as He saith: "Verily, the sun and the moon are both condemned to the torment of infernal fire."[1] You are no doubt familiar with the interpretation of the term "sun" and "moon" mentioned in this verse; no need therefore to refer unto it. And whosoever is of the element of this "sun" and "moon", that is, followeth the example of these leaders in setting his face

[1] Qur'án 55:5.

towards falsehood and in turning away from the truth he undoubtedly cometh out of infernal gloom and returneth thereunto.

And now, O seeker, it behooveth us firmly to cling unto the 'Urvatu'l-Vuthqá, that perchance we may leave behind the darksome night of error, and embrace the dawning light of divine guidance. Shall we not flee from the face of denial, and seek the sheltering shadow of certitude? Shall we not free ourselves from the horror of satanic gloom, and hasten towards the rising light of the heavenly Beauty? In such wise, we bestow upon you the fruit of the Tree of divine knowledge, that ye may gladly and joyously abide in the Riḍván of divine wisdom.

In another sense, by the terms 'sun', 'moon', and 'stars' are meant such laws and teachings as have been established and proclaimed in every Dispensation, such as the laws of prayer and fasting. These have, according to the law of the Qur'án, been regarded, when the beauty of the Prophet Muḥammad had passed beyond the veil, as the most fundamental and binding laws of His dispensation. To this testify the texts of the traditions and chronicles, which, on account of their being widely known, need not be referred to here. Nay rather, in every Dispensation the law concerning prayer hath been emphasized and universally enforced. To this testify the recorded traditions ascribed to the lights that have emanated from the Day-star of Truth, the essence of the Prophet Muḥammad.

The traditions established the fact that in all Dispensations the law of prayer hath constituted a fundamental element of the Revelation of all the Prophets of God—a law the form and the manner of which hath been adapted to the varying requirements of every age. Inasmuch as every subsequent Revelation hath abolished the manners, habits, and teachings that have been clearly, specifically, and firmly established by the former Dispensation, these have accordingly been symbolically expressed in terms of 'sun' and 'moon'. "That He might prove you, which of you excel in deeds." [1]

Moreover, in the traditions the terms "sun" and "moon" have been applied to prayer and fasting, even as it is said: "Fasting is illumination, prayer is light." One day, a well-known divine came to

[1] Qur'án 67:2.

visit Us. While We were conversing with him, he referred to the above-quoted tradition. He said: "Inasmuch as fasting causeth the heat of the body to increase, it hath therefore been likened unto the light of the sun; and as the prayer of the night-season refresheth man, it hath been compared unto the radiance of the moon." Thereupon We realized that that poor man had not been favoured with a single drop of the ocean of true understanding, and had strayed far from the burning Bush of divine wisdom. We then politely observed to him saying: "The interpretation your honour hath given to this tradition is the one current amongst the people. Could it not be interpreted differently?" He asked Us: "What could it be?" We made reply: "Muḥammad, the Seal of the Prophets, and the most distinguished of God's chosen Ones, hath likened the Dispensation of the Qur'án unto heaven, by reason of its loftiness, its paramount influence, its majesty, and the fact that it comprehendeth all religions. And as the sun and moon constitute the brightest and most prominent luminaries in the heavens, similarly in the heaven of the religion of God two shining orbs have been ordained—fasting and prayer. 'Islám is heaven; fasting is its sun, prayer, its moon.'"

This is the purpose underlying the symbolic words of the Manifestations of God. Consequently, the application of the terms "sun" and "moon" to the things already mentioned hath been demonstrated and justified by the text of the sacred verses and the recorded traditions. Hence, it is clear and manifest that by the words "the sun shall be darkened, and the moon shall not give her light, and the stars shall fall from heaven" is intended the waywardness of the divines, and the annulment of laws firmly established by divine Revelation, all of which, in symbolic language, have been foreshadowed by the Manifestation of God. None except the righteous shall partake of this cup, none but the godly can share therein. "The righteous shall drink of a cup tempered at the camphor fountain." [1]

It is unquestionable that in every succeeding Revelation the "sun" and "moon" of the teachings, laws, commandments, and prohibitions which have been established in the preceding Dispensation, and which have overshadowed the people of that age, become darkened, that is, are exhausted, and cease to exert their influence. Consider now,

[1] Qur'án 76:5.

had the people of the Gospel recognized the meaning of the symbolic terms "sun" and "moon," had they sought, unlike the froward and perverse, enlightenment from Him Who is the Revealer of divine knowledge, they would have surely comprehended the purpose of these terms, and would not have become afflicted and oppressed by the darkness of their selfish desires. Yea, but since they have failed to acquire true knowledge from its very Source, they have perished in the perilous vale of waywardness and misbelief. They still have not awakened to perceive that all the signs foretold have been made manifest, that the promised Sun hath risen above the horizon of divine Revelation, and that the "sun" and "moon" of the teachings, the laws, and learning of a former Dispensation have darkened and set.

And now, with fixed gaze and steady wings enter thou the way of certitude and truth. "Say: It is God; then leave them to entertain themselves with their cavilings." [1] Thus, wilt thou be accounted of those companions of whom He saith: "They that say 'Our Lord is God,' and continue steadfast in His way, upon them, verily, shall the

[1] Qur'án 6:91.

angels descend." [1] Then shalt thou witness all these mysteries with thine own eyes.

O my brother! Take thou the step of the spirit, so that, swift as the twinkling of an eye, thou mayest flash through the wilds of remoteness and bereavement, attain the Riḍván of everlasting reunion, and in one breath commune with the heavenly Spirits. For with human feet thou canst never hope to traverse these immeasurable distances, nor attain thy goal. Peace be upon him whom the light of truth guideth unto all truth, and who, in the name of God, standeth in the path of His Cause, upon the shore of true understanding.

This is the meaning of the sacred verse: "But nay! I swear by the Lord of the Easts and the Wests," [2] inasmuch as the "Suns" referred to have each their own particular rising and setting place. And as the commentators of the Qur'án have failed to grasp the symbolic meaning of these "Suns," they therefore were at pains to interpret the above-quoted verse. Some of them maintained that owing to the fact that the sun each day rises from a differ-

[1] Qur'án 41:30.
[2] Qur'án 70:40.

ent point, the terms "easts" and "wests" have been mentioned in the plural. Others have written that by this verse the four seasons of the year are intended, inasmuch as the dawning and setting points of the sun vary with the change of the seasons. Such is the depth of their understanding! None the less, they persist in imputing error and folly to those Gems of knowledge, those irreproachable and purest Symbols of wisdom.

In like manner, strive thou to comprehend from these lucid, these powerful, conclusive, and unequivocal statements the meaning of the "cleaving of the heaven"—one of the signs that must needs herald the coming of the last Hour, the Day of Resurrection. As He hath said: "When the heaven shall be cloven asunder." [1] By "heaven" is meant the heaven of divine Revelation, which is elevated with every Manifestation, and rent asunder with every subsequent one. By "cloven asunder" is meant that the former Dispensation is superseded and annulled. I swear by God! That this heaven being cloven asunder is, to the discerning, an act mightier than the cleaving of the skies! Ponder a while. That a divine Revelation which for years

[1] Qur'án 82:1.

hath been securely established; beneath whose shadow all who have embraced it have been reared and nurtured; by the light of whose law generations of men have been disciplined; the excellency of whose word men have heard recounted by their fathers; in such wise that human eye hath beheld naught but the pervading influence of its grace, and mortal ear hath heard naught but the resounding majesty of its command—what act is mightier than that such a Revelation should, by the power of God, be "cloven asunder" and be abolished at the appearance of one soul? Reflect, is this a mightier act than that which these abject and foolish men have imagined the "cleaving of the heaven" to mean?

Moreover, consider the hardships and the bitterness of the lives of those Revealers of the divine Beauty. Reflect, how single-handed and alone they faced the world and all its peoples, and promulgated the Law of God! No matter how severe the persecutions inflicted upon those holy, those precious, and tender Souls, they still remained, in the plenitude of their power, patient, and, despite their ascendancy, they suffered and endured.

In like manner, endeavour to comprehend the meaning of the "changing of the earth." Know thou, that upon whatever hearts the bountiful showers of mercy, raining from the "heaven" of divine Revelation, have fallen, the earth of those hearts hath verily been changed into the earth of divine knowledge and wisdom. What myrtles of unity hath the soil of their hearts produced! What blossoms of true knowledge and wisdom hath their illumined bosoms yielded! Were the earth of their hearts to remain unchanged, how could such souls who have not been taught one letter, have seen no teacher, and entered no school, utter such words and display such knowledge as none can apprehend? Methinks they have been moulded from the clay of infinite knowledge, and kneaded with the water of divine wisdom. Therefore, hath it been said: "Knowledge is a light which God casteth into the heart of whomsoever He willeth." It is this kind of knowledge which is and hath ever been praiseworthy, and not the limited knowledge that hath sprung forth from veiled and obscured minds. This limited knowledge they even stealthily borrow one from the other, and vainly pride themselves therein!

Would that the hearts of men could be cleansed from these man-made limitations and obscure thoughts imposed upon them! haply they may be illumined by the light of the Sun of true knowledge, and comprehend the mysteries of divine wisdom. Consider now, were the parched and barren soil of these hearts to remain unchanged, how could they ever become the Recipients of the revelation of the mysteries of God, and the Revealers of the divine Essence? Thus hath He said: "On the day when the earth shall be changed into another earth." [1]

The breeze of the bounty of the King of creation hath caused even the physical earth to be changed, were ye to ponder in your hearts the mysteries of divine Revelation.

And now, comprehend the meaning of this verse: "The whole earth shall on the Resurrection Day be but His handful, and in His right hand shall the heavens be folded together. Praise be to Him! and high be He uplifted above the partners they join with him!" [2] And now, be fair in thy judgment. Were this verse to have the meaning which men suppose it to have, of what profit, one

[1] Qur'án 14:48.
[2] Qur'án 39:67.

may ask, could it be to man? Moreover, it is evident and manifest that no such hand as could be seen by human eye could accomplish such deeds, or could possibly be ascribed to the exalted Essence of the one true God. Nay, to acknowledge such a thing is naught but sheer blasphemy, an utter perversion of the truth. And should it be supposed that by this verse are meant the Manifestations of God, Who will be called upon, on the Day of Judgment, to perform such deeds, this too seemeth far from the truth, and is surely of no profit. On the contrary, by the term "earth" is meant the earth of understanding and knowledge, and by "heavens" the heavens of divine Revelation. Reflect thou, how, in one hand, He hath, by His mighty grasp, turned the earth of knowledge and understanding, previously unfolded, into a mere handful, and, on the other, spread out a new and highly exalted earth in the hearts of men, thus causing the freshest and loveliest blossoms, and the mightiest and loftiest trees to spring forth from the illumined bosom of man.

In like manner, reflect how the elevated heavens of the Dispensations of the past have, in the right hand of power, been folded together, how the heavens of divine Revelation have been raised by the command of God, and been adorned by the sun, the moon, and stars of His wondrous commandments. Such are the mysteries of the Word of God, which have been unveiled and made manifest, that haply thou mayest apprehend the morning light of divine guidance, mayest quench, by the power of reliance and renunciation, the lamp of idle fancy, of vain imaginings, of hesitation, and doubt, and mayest kindle, in the inmost chamber of thine heart, the new-born light of divine knowledge and certitude.

Know verily that the purpose underlying all these symbolic terms and abstruse allusions, which emanate from the Revealers of God's holy Cause, hath been to test and prove the peoples of the world; that thereby the earth of the pure and illuminated hearts may be known from the perishable and barren soil. From time immemorial such hath been the way of God amidst His creatures, and to this testify the records of the sacred books.

And likewise, reflect upon the revealed verse concerning the "Qiblih." [1] When Muhammad,

[1] The direction toward which the face must be turned when praying.

the Sun of Prophethood, had fled from the day-spring of Baṭḥá [1] unto Yaṯẖrib, [2] He continued to turn His face, while praying, unto Jerusalem, the holy city, until the time when the Jews began to utter unseemly words against Him—words which if mentioned would ill befit these pages and would weary the reader. Muḥammad strongly resented these words. Whilst, wrapt in meditation and wonder, He was gazing toward heaven, He heard the kindly Voice of Gabriel, saying: "We behold Thee from above, turning Thy face to heaven; but We will have Thee turn to a Qiblih which shall please Thee." [3] On a subsequent day, when the Prophet, together with His companions, was offering the noontide prayer, and had already performed two of the prescribed Rik'ats, [4] the Voice of Gabriel was heard again: "Turn Thou Thy face towards the sacred Mosque." [5, 6] In the midst of that same prayer, Muḥammad suddenly turned His face away from Jerusalem and faced the Ka'bih. Whereupon, a profound dismay seized suddenly the companions of the Prophet. Their faith was

[1] Mecca.
[2] Medina.
[3] Qur'án 2:144.
[4] Prostrations.
[5] At Mecca.
[6] Qur'án 2:149.

shaken severely. So great was their alarm, that many of them, discontinuing their prayer, apostatized their faith. Verily, God caused not this turmoil but to test and prove His servants. Otherwise, He, the ideal King, could easily have left the Qiblih unchanged, and could have caused Jerusalem to remain the Point of Adoration unto His Dispensation, thereby withholding not from that holy city the distinction of acceptance which had been conferred upon it.

None of the many Prophets sent down, since Moses was made manifest, as Messengers of the Word of God, such as David, Jesus, and others among the more exalted Manifestations who have appeared during the intervening period between the Revelations of Moses and Muḥammad, ever altered the law of the Qiblih. These Messengers of the Lord of creation have, one and all, directed their peoples to turn unto the same direction. In the eyes of God, the ideal King, all the places of the earth are one and the same, excepting that place which, in the days of His Manifestations, He doth appoint for a particular purpose. Even as He hath revealed: "The East and the West are God's: therefore whichever way ye turn, there is the face of God." [1] Notwithstanding the truth of these facts, why should the Qiblih have been changed, thus casting such dismay amongst the people, causing the companions of the Prophet to waver, and throwing so great a confusion into their midst? Yea, such things as throw consternation into the hearts of all men come to pass only that each soul may be tested by the touchstone of God, that the true may be known and distinguished from the false. Thus hath He revealed after the breach amongst the people: "We did not appoint that which Thou wouldst have to be the Qiblih, but that We might know him who followeth the Apostle from him who turneth on his heels." [2] "Affrighted asses fleeing from a lion." [3]

Were you to ponder, but for a while, these utterances in your heart, you would surely find the portals of understanding unlocked before your face, and would behold all knowledge and the mysteries thereof unveiled before your eyes. Such things take place only that the souls of men may develop and be delivered from the prison-cage of self and desire. Otherwise, that ideal King hath, throughout

[1] Qur'án 2:115.
[2] Qur'án 2:143.
[3] Qur'án 74:50.

eternity, been in His Essence independent of the comprehension of all beings, and will continue, for ever, in His own Being to be exalted above the adoration of every soul. A single breeze of His affluence doth suffice to adorn all mankind with the robe of wealth; and one drop out of the ocean of His bountiful grace is enough to confer upon all beings the glory of everlasting life. But inasmuch as the divine Purpose hath decreed that the true should be known from the false, and the sun from the shadow, He hath, therefore, in every season sent down upon mankind the showers of tests from His realm of glory.

Were men to meditate upon the lives of the Prophets of old, so easily would they come to know and understand the ways of these Prophets that they would cease to be veiled by such deeds and words as are contrary to their own worldly desires, and thus consume every intervening veil with the fire burning in the Bush of divine knowledge, and abide secure upon the throne of peace and certitude. For instance, consider Moses, son of 'Imrán, one of the exalted Prophets and Author of a divinely-revealed Book. Whilst passing, one day, through the market, in His early days, ere His

ministry was proclaimed, He saw two men engaged
in fighting. One of them asked the help of Moses
against his opponent. Whereupon, Moses inter-
vened and slew him. To this testifieth the record
of the sacred Book. Should the details be cited,
they will lengthen and interrupt the course of the
argument. The report of this incident spread
throughout the city, and Moses was full of fear,
as is witnessed by the text of the Book. And when
the warning: "O Moses! of a truth, the chiefs take
counsel to slay Thee" [1] reached His ears, He went
forth from the city, and sojourned in Midian in
the service of Shoeb. While returning, Moses entered the holy vale, situate in the wilderness of
Sinai, and there beheld the vision of the King of
glory from the "Tree that belongeth neither to the
East nor to the West."[2] There He heard the soul-
stirring Voice of the Spirit speaking from out of
the kindled Fire, bidding Him to shed upon Pha-
raonic souls the light of divine guidance; so that,
liberating them from the shadows of the valley of
self and desire, He might enable them to attain
the meads of heavenly delight, and delivering
them, through the Salsabíl of renunciation, from
the bewilderment of remoteness, cause them to en-

[1] Qur'án 28:20.   [2] Qur'án 24:35.

ter the peaceful city of the divine presence. When
Moses came unto Pharaoh and delivered unto him,
as bidden by God, the divine Message, Pharaoh
spoke insultingly saying: "Art thou not he that
committed murder, and became an infidel?" Thus
recounted the Lord of majesty as having been said
by Pharaoh unto Moses: "What a deed is that
which Thou hast done! Thou art one of the un-
grateful. He said: 'I did it indeed, and I was one
of those who erred. And I fled from you when I
feared you, but My Lord hath given Me wisdom,
and hath made Me one of His Apostles.'" [1]

And now ponder in thy heart the commotion
which God stirreth up. Reflect upon the strange
and manifold trials with which He doth test His
servants. Consider how He hath suddenly chosen
from among His servants, and entrusted with the
exalted mission of divine guidance Him Who was
known as guilty of homicide, Who, Himself, had
acknowledged His cruelty, and Who for well-nigh
thirty years had, in the eyes of the world, been
reared in the home of Pharaoh and been nourished
at his table. Was not God, the omnipotent King,
able to withhold the hand of Moses from murder,

[1] Qur'án 26:19.

so that manslaughter should not be attributed unto
Him, causing bewilderment and aversion among
the people?

Likewise, reflect upon the state and condition of
Mary. So deep was the perplexity of that most
beauteous countenance, so grievous her case, that
she bitterly regretted she had ever been born. To
this beareth witness the text of the sacred verse
wherein it is mentioned that after Mary had given
birth to Jesus, she bemoaned her plight and cried
out: "O would that I had died ere this, and been
a thing forgotten, forgotten quite!"[1] I swear by
God! Such lamenting consumeth the heart and
shaketh the being. Such consternation of soul, such
despondency, could have been caused by no other
than the censure of the enemy and the cavilings
of the infidel and perverse. Reflect, what answer
could Mary have given to the people around her?
How could she claim that a Babe Whose father
was unknown had been conceived of the Holy
Ghost? Therefore did Mary, that veiled and immortal Countenance, take up her Child and return
unto her home. No sooner had the eyes of the
people fallen upon her than they raised their voice

[1] Qur'án 19:22.

saying: "O sister of Aaron! Thy father was not a man of wickedness, nor unchaste thy mother." [1]

And now, meditate upon this most great convulsion, this grievous test. Notwithstanding all these things, God conferred upon that essence of the Spirit, Who was known amongst the people as fatherless, the glory of Prophethood, and made Him His testimony unto all that are in heaven and on earth.

Behold how contrary are the ways of the Manifestations of God, as ordained by the King of creation, to the ways and desires of men! As thou comest to comprehend the essence of these divine mysteries, thou wilt grasp the purpose of God, the divine Charmer, the Best-Beloved. Thou wilt regard the words and the deeds of that almighty Sovereign as one and the same; in such wise that whatsoever thou dost behold in His deeds, the same wilt thou find in His sayings, and whatsoever thou dost read in His sayings, that wilt thou recognize in His deeds. Thus it is that outwardly such deeds and words are the fire of vengeance unto the wicked, and inwardly the waters of mercy unto the righteous. Were the eye of the heart to open, it

[1] Qur'án 19:28.

would surely perceive that the words revealed from the heaven of the will of God are at one with, and the same as, the deeds that have emanated from the Kingdom of divine power.

And now, take heed, O brother! If such things be revealed in this Dispensation, and such incidents come to pass, at the present time, what would the people do? I swear by Him Who is the true Educator of mankind and the Revealer of the Word of God that the people would instantly and unquestionably pronounce Him an infidel and would sentence Him to death. How far are they from hearkening unto the voice that declareth: Lo! a Jesus hath appeared out of the breath of the Holy Ghost, and a Moses summoned to a divinely-appointed task! Were a myriad voices to be raised, no ear would listen if We said that upon a fatherless Child hath been conferred the mission of Prophethood, or that a murderer hath brought from the flame of the burning Bush the message of "Verily, verily, I am God!"

If the eye of justice be opened, it will readily recognize, in the light of that which hath been mentioned, that He, Who is the Cause and ultimate Purpose of all these things, is made manifest in this day. Though similar events have not occurred in this Dispensation, yet the people still cling to such vain imaginings as are cherished by the reprobate. How grievous the charges brought against Him! How severe the persecutions inflicted upon Him—charges and persecutions the like of which men have neither seen nor heard!

Great God! When the stream of utterance reached this stage, We beheld, and lo! the sweet savours of God were being wafted from the day-spring of Revelation, and the morning breeze was blowing out of the Sheba of the Eternal. Its tidings rejoiced anew the heart, and imparted immeasurable gladness to the soul. It made all things new, and brought unnumbered and inestimable gifts from the unknowable Friend. The robe of human praise can never hope to match Its noble stature, and Its shining figure the mantle of utterance can never fit. Without word It unfoldeth the inner mysteries, and without speech It revealeth the secrets of the divine sayings. It teacheth lamentation and moaning to the nightingales warbling upon the bough of remoteness and bereavement, instructeth them in the art of love's ways, and showeth them the secret of heart-surrender To the

flowers of the Riḍván of heavenly reunion It revealeth the endearments of the impassioned lover,
and unveileth the charm of the fair. Upon the
anemones of the garden of love It bestoweth the
mysteries of truth, and within the breasts of lovers
It entrusteth the symbols of the innermost subtleties. At this hour, so liberal is the outpouring of
Its grace that the holy Spirit itself is envious! It
hath imparted to the drop the waves of the sea, and
endowed the mote with the splendour of the sun.
So great are the overflowings of Its bounty that the
foulest beetle hath sought the perfume of the musk,
and the bat the light of the sun. It hath quickened
the dead with the breath of life, and caused them to
speed out of the sepulchres of their mortal bodies.
It hath established the ignorant upon the seats of
learning, and elevated the oppressor to the throne
of justice.

The universe is pregnant with these manifold
bounties, awaiting the hour when the effects of Its
unseen gifts will be made manifest in this world,
when the languishing and sore athirst will attain
the living Kawthar of their Well-Beloved, and the
erring wanderer, lost in the wilds of remoteness
and nothingness, will enter the tabernacle of life,

and attain reunion with his heart's desire. In the soil of whose heart will these holy seeds germinate? From the garden of whose soul will the blossoms of the invisible realities spring forth? Verily, I say, so fierce is the blaze of the Bush of love, burning in the Sinai of the heart, that the streaming waters of holy utterance can never quench its flame. Oceans can never allay this Leviathan's burning thirst, and this Phoenix of the undying fire can abide nowhere save in the glow of the countenance of the Well-Beloved. Therefore, O brother! kindle with the oil of wisdom the lamp of the spirit within the innermost chamber of thy heart, and guard it with the globe of understanding, that the breath of the infidel may extinguish not its flame nor dim its brightness. Thus have We illuminated the heavens of utterance with the splendours of the Sun of divine wisdom and understanding, that thy heart may find peace, that thou mayest be of those who, on the wings of certitude, have soared unto the heaven of the love of their Lord, the All-Merciful.

And now, concerning His words: "And then shall appear the sign of the Son of man in heaven." By these words it is meant that when the sun of the heavenly teachings hath been eclipsed, the stars of the divinely-established laws have fallen, and the moon of true knowledge—the educator of mankind—hath been obscured; when the standards of guidance and felicity have been reversed, and the morn of truth and righteousness hath sunk in night, then shall the sign of the Son of man appear in heaven. By "heaven" is meant the visible heaven, inasmuch as when the hour draweth nigh on which the Day-star of the heaven of justice shall be made manifest, and the Ark of divine guidance shall sail upon the sea of glory, a star will appear in the heaven, heralding unto its people the advent of that most great light. In like manner, in the invisible heaven a star shall be made manifest who, unto the peoples of the earth, shall act as a harbinger of the break of that true and exalted Morn. These twofold signs, in the visible and the invisible heaven, have announced the Revelation of each of the Prophets of God, as is commonly believed.

Among the Prophets was Abraham, the Friend of God. Ere He manifested Himself, Nimrod dreamed a dream. Thereupon, he summoned the soothsayers, who informed him of the rise of a star in the heaven. Likewise, there appeared a herald who announced throughout the land the coming of Abraham.

After Him came Moses, He Who held converse with God. The soothsayers of His time warned Pharaoh in these terms: "A star hath risen in the heaven, and lo! it foreshadoweth the conception of a Child Who holdeth your fate and the fate of your people in His hand." In like manner, there appeared a sage who, in the darkness of the night, brought tidings of joy unto the people of Israel, imparting consolation to their souls, and assurance to their hearts. To this testify the records of the sacred books. Were the details to be mentioned, this epistle would swell into a book. Moreover, it is not Our wish to relate the stories of the days that are past. God is Our witness that what We even now mention is due solely to Our tender affection for thee, that haply the poor of the earth may attain the shores of the sea of wealth, the ignorant be led unto the ocean of divine knowledge, and they that thirst for understanding partake of the Salsabíl of divine wisdom. Otherwise, this servant regardeth the consideration of such records a grave mistake and a grievous transgression.

In like manner, when the hour of the Revelation of Jesus drew nigh, a few of the Magi, aware that the star of Jesus had appeared in heaven, sought and followed it, till they came unto the city which was the seat of the Kingdom of Herod. The sway of his sovereignty in those days embraced the whole of that land.

These Magi said: "Where is He that is born King of the Jews? for we have seen His star in the east and are come to worship Him!" [1] When they had searched, they found out that in Bethlehem, in the land of Judea, the Child had been born. This was the sign that was manifested in the visible heaven. As to the sign in the invisible heaven—the heaven of divine knowledge and understanding—it was Yaḥyá, son of Zachariah, who gave unto the people the tidings of the Manifestation of Jesus. Even as He hath revealed: "God announceth Yaḥyá to thee, who shall bear witness unto the Word from God, and a great one and chaste." [2] By the term "Word" is meant Jesus, Whose coming Yaḥyá foretold. Moreover, in the heavenly Scriptures it is written: "John the Baptist was preaching in the wilderness of Judea, and

[1] Matthew 2:2.
[2] Qur'án 3:39.

[64]

saying, Repent ye: for the Kingdom of heaven is at hand." [1] By John is meant Yaḥyá.

Likewise, ere the beauty of Muḥammad was unveiled, the signs of the visible heaven were made manifest. As to the signs of the invisible heaven, there appeared four men who successively announced unto the people the joyful tidings of the rise of that divine Luminary. Rúz-bih, later named Salmán, was honoured by being in their service. As the end of one of these approached, he would send Rúz-bih unto the other, until the fourth who, feeling his death to be nigh, addressed Rúz-bih saying: "O Rúz-bih! when thou hast taken up my body and buried it, go to Ḥijáz for there the Daystar of Muḥammad will arise. Happy art thou, for thou shalt behold His face!"

And now concerning this wondrous and most exalted Cause. Know thou verily that many an astronomer hath announced the appearance of its star in the visible heaven. Likewise, there appeared on earth Aḥmad and Káẓim,[2] those twin resplendent lights—may God sanctify their resting-place!

[1] Matthew 3:1-2.
[2] Shaykh Aḥmad-i-Aḥsá'í and Siyyid Káẓim-i-Rashtí.

[65]

From all that We have stated it hath become clear and manifest that before the revelation of each of the Mirrors reflecting the divine Essence, the signs heralding their advent must needs be revealed in the visible heaven as well as in the invisible, wherein is the seat of the sun of knowledge, of the moon of wisdom, and of the stars of understanding and utterance. The sign of the invisible heaven must needs be revealed in the person of that perfect man who, before each Manifestation appeareth, educateth, and prepareth the souls of men for the advent of the divine Luminary, the Light of the unity of God amongst men.

And now, with reference to His words: "And then shall all the tribes of the earth mourn, and they shall see the Son of man coming in the clouds of heaven with power and great glory." These words signify that in those days men will lament the loss of the Sun of the divine beauty, of the Moon of knowledge, and of the Stars of divine wisdom. Thereupon, they will behold the countenance of the promised One, the adored Beauty, descending from heaven and riding upon the clouds. By this is meant that the divine Beauty will be made manifest from the heaven of the will of God, and will appear in the form of the human temple. The term "heaven" denoteth loftiness and exaltation, inasmuch as it is the seat of the revelation of those Manifestations of Holiness, the Day-springs of ancient glory. These ancient Beings, though delivered from the womb of their mother, have in reality descended from the heaven of the will of God. Though they be dwelling on this earth, yet their true habitations are the retreats of glory in the realms above. Whilst walking amongst mortals, they soar in the heaven of the divine presence. Without feet they tread the path of the spirit, and without wings they rise unto the exalted heights of divine unity. With every fleeting breath they cover the immensity of space, and at every moment traverse the kingdoms of the visible and the invisible. Upon their thrones is written: "Nothing whatsoever keepeth Him from being occupied with any other thing;" and on their seats is inscribed: "Verily, His ways differ every day." [1] They are sent forth through the transcendent power of the Ancient of Days, and are raised up by the exalted will of God, the most mighty King. This is what is meant by the words: "coming in the clouds of heaven."

[1] Qur'án 55:29.

In the utterances of the divine Luminaries the term "heaven" hath been applied to many and divers things; such as the "heaven of Command," the "heaven of Will," the "heaven of the divine Purpose," the "heaven of divine Knowledge," the "heaven of Certitude," the "heaven of Utterance," the "heaven of Revelation," the "heaven of Concealment," and the like. In every instance, He hath given the term "heaven" a special meaning, the significance of which is revealed to none save those that have been initiated into the divine mysteries, and have drunk from the chalice of immortal life. For example, He saith: "The heaven hath sustenance for you, and it containeth that which you are promised;" [1] whereas it is the earth that yieldeth such sustenance. Likewise, it hath been said: "The names come down from heaven;" whereas they proceed out of the mouth of men. Wert thou to cleanse the mirror of thy heart from the dust of malice, thou wouldst apprehend the meaning of the symbolic terms revealed by the all-embracing Word of God made manifest in every Dispensation, and wouldst discover the mysteries of divine knowledge. Not, however, until thou consumest with the flame of utter detachment those veils of

[1] Qur'án 51:22.

idle learning, that are current amongst men, canst thou behold the resplendent morn of true knowledge.

Know verily that Knowledge is of two kinds: Divine and Satanic. The one welleth out from the fountain of divine inspiration; the other is but a reflection of vain and obscure thoughts. The source of the former is God Himself; the motive-force of the latter the whisperings of selfish desire. The one is guided by the principle: "Fear ye God; God will teach you;"[1] the other is but a confirmation of the truth: "Knowledge is the most grievous veil between man and his Creator." The former bringeth forth the fruit of patience, of longing desire, of true understanding, and love; whilst the latter can yield naught but arrogance, vainglory and conceit. From the sayings of those Masters of holy utterance, Who have expounded the meaning of true knowledge, the odour of these dark teachings, which have obscured the world, can in no wise be detected. The tree of such teachings can yield no result except iniquity and rebellion, and beareth no fruit but hatred and envy. Its fruit is deadly poison; its shadow a consuming fire. How well hath it been said: "Cling unto the robe of the Desire of

[1] Qur'án 2:282.

[69]

thy heart, and put thou away all shame; bid the worldlywise be gone, however great their name."

The heart must needs therefore be cleansed from the idle sayings of men, and sanctified from every earthly affection, so that it may discover the hidden meaning of divine inspiration, and become the treasury of the mysteries of divine knowledge. Thus hath it been said: "He that treadeth the snow-white Path, and followeth in the footsteps of the Crimson Pillar, shall never attain unto his abode unless his hands are empty of those worldly things cherished by men." This is the prime requisite of whosoever treadeth this path. Ponder thereon, that, with eyes unveiled, thou mayest perceive the truth of these words.

We have digressed from the purpose of Our argument, although whatsoever is mentioned serveth only to confirm Our purpose. By God! however great Our desire to be brief, yet We feel We cannot restrain Our pen. Notwithstanding all that We have mentioned, how innumerable are the pearls which have remained unpierced in the shell of Our heart! How many the ḥúrís of inner meaning that are as yet concealed within the chambers of divine wisdom! None hath yet approached them;—ḥúrís, "whom no man nor spirit hath touched before." [1] Notwithstanding all that hath been said, it seemeth as if not one letter of Our purpose hath been uttered, nor a single sign divulged concerning Our object. When will a faithful seeker be found who will don the garb of pilgrimage, attain the Ka'bih of the heart's desire, and, without ear or tongue, discover the mysteries of divine utterance?

By these luminous, these conclusive, and lucid statements, the meaning of "heaven" in the aforementioned verse hath thus been made clear and evident. And now regarding His words, that the Son of man shall "come in the clouds of heaven." By the term "clouds" is meant those things that are contrary to the ways and desires of men. Even as He hath revealed in the verse already quoted: "As oft as an Apostle cometh unto you with that which your souls desire not, ye swell with pride, accusing some of being impostors and slaying others." [2] These "clouds" signify, in one sense, the annulment of laws, the abrogation of former Dispensations, the repeal of rituals and customs current

[1] Qur'án 55:56.
[2] Qur'án 2:87.

amongst men, the exalting of the illiterate faithful above the learned opposers of the Faith. In another sense, they mean the appearance of that immortal Beauty in the image of mortal man, with such human limitations as eating and drinking, poverty and riches, glory and abasement, sleeping and waking, and such other things as cast doubt in the minds of men, and cause them to turn away. All such veils are symbolically referred to as "clouds."

These are the "clouds" that cause the heavens of the knowledge and understanding of all that dwell on earth to be cloven asunder. Even as He hath revealed: "On that day shall the heaven be cloven by the clouds."[1] Even as the clouds prevent the eyes of men from beholding the sun, so do these things hinder the souls of men from recognizing the light of the divine Luminary. To this beareth witness that which hath proceeded out of the mouth of the unbelievers as revealed in the sacred Book: "And they have said: 'What manner of apostle is this? He eateth food, and walketh the streets. Unless an angel be sent down and take part in His warnings, we will not believe.'"[2] Other

[1] Qur'án 25:25.
[2] Qur'án 25:7.

Prophets, similarly, have been subject to poverty and afflictions, to hunger, and to the ills and chances of this world. As these holy Persons were subject to such needs and wants, the people were, consequently, lost in the wilds of misgivings and doubts, and were afflicted with bewilderment and perplexity. How, they wondered, could such a person be sent down from God, assert His ascendancy over all the peoples and kindreds of the earth, and claim Himself to be the goal of all creation,— even as He hath said: "But for Thee, I would not have created all that are in heaven and on earth," —and yet be subject to such trivial things? You must undoubtedly have been informed of the tribulations, the poverty, the ills, and the degradation that have befallen every Prophet of God and His companions. You must have heard how the heads of their followers were sent as presents unto different cities, how grievously they were hindered from that whereunto they were commanded. Each and every one of them fell a prey to the hands of the enemies of His Cause, and had to suffer whatsoever they decreed.

It is evident that the changes brought about in every Dispensation constitute the dark clouds that

intervene between the eye of man's understanding
and the divine Luminary which shineth forth from
the dayspring of the divine Essence. Consider how
men for generations have been blindly imitating
their fathers, and have been trained according to
such ways and manners as have been laid down by
the dictates of their Faith. Were these men, therefore, to discover suddenly that a Man, Who hath
been living in their midst, Who, with respect to
every human limitation, hath been their equal, had
risen to abolish every established principle imposed by their Faith—principles by which for
centuries they have been disciplined, and every
opposer and denier of which they have come to regard as infidel, profligate and wicked,—they would
of a certainty be veiled and hindered from
acknowledging His truth. Such things are as
"clouds" that veil the eyes of those whose inner
being hath not tasted the Salsabíl of detachment,
nor drunk from the Kawthar of the knowledge of
God. Such men, when acquainted with these circumstances, become so veiled that without the least
question, they pronounce the Manifestation of God
an infidel, and sentence Him to death. You must
have heard of such things taking place all down
the ages, and are now observing them in these days.

It behooveth us, therefore, to make the utmost endeavour, that, by God's invisible assistance, these dark veils, these clouds of Heaven-sent trials, may not hinder us from beholding the beauty of His shining Countenance, and that we may recognize Him only by His own Self. And should we ask for a testimony of His truth, we should content ourselves with one, and only one; that thereby we may attain unto Him Who is the Fountain-head of infinite grace, and in Whose presence all the world's abundance fadeth into nothingness, that we may cease to cavil at Him every day and to cleave unto our own idle fancy.

Gracious God! Notwithstanding the warning which, in marvelously symbolic language and subtle allusions, hath been uttered in days past, and which was intended to awaken the peoples of the world and to prevent them from being deprived of their share of the billowing ocean of God's grace, yet such things as have already been witnessed have come to pass! Reference to these things hath also been made in the Qur'án, as witnessed by this verse: "What can such expect but that God should come down to them overshadowed with clouds?" [1]

[1] Qur'án 2:210.

A number of the divines, who hold firmly to the letter of the Word of God, have come to regard this verse as one of the signs of that expected resurrection which is born of their idle fancy. This, notwithstanding the fact that similar references have been made in most of the heavenly Books, and have been recorded in all the passages connected with the signs of the coming Manifestation.

Likewise, He saith: "On the day when the heaven shall give out a palpable smoke, which shall enshroud mankind: this will be an afflictive torment." [1] The All-Glorious hath decreed these very things, that are contrary to the desires of wicked men, to be the touchstone and standard whereby He proveth His servants, that the just may be known from the wicked, and the faithful distinguished from the infidel. The symbolic term "smoke" denotes grave dissensions, the abrogation and demolition of recognized standards, and the utter destruction of their narrow-minded exponents. What smoke more dense and overpowering than the one which hath now enshrouded all the peoples of the world, which hath become a torment

[1] Qur'án 44:10.

[76]

unto them, and from which they hopelessly fail to deliver themselves, however much they strive? So fierce is this fire of self burning within them, that at every moment they seem to be afflicted with fresh torments. The more they are told that this wondrous Cause of God, this Revelation from the Most High, hath been made manifest to all mankind, and is waxing greater and stronger every day, the fiercer groweth the blaze of the fire in their hearts. The more they observe the indomitable strength, the sublime renunciation, the unwavering constancy of God's holy companions, who, by the aid of God, are growing nobler and more glorious every day, the deeper the dismay which ravageth their souls. In these days, praise be to God, the power of His Word hath obtained such ascendancy over men, that they dare breathe no word. Were they to encounter one of the companions of God who, if he could, would, freely and joyously, offer up ten thousand lives as a sacrifice for his Beloved, so great would be their fear, that they forthwith would profess their faith in Him, whilst privily they would vilify and execrate His name! Even as He hath revealed: "And when they meet you, they say, 'We believe'; but when they are apart, they bite their fingers' ends at you, out of wrath. Say:

'Die in your wrath!' God truly knoweth the very recesses of your breasts."[1]

Ere long, thine eyes will behold the standards of divine power unfurled throughout all regions, and the signs of His triumphant might and sovereignty manifest in every land. As most of the divines have failed to apprehend the meaning of these verses, and have not grasped the significance of the Day of Resurrection, they therefore have foolishly interpreted these verses according to their idle and faulty conception. The one true God is My witness! Little perception is required to enable them to gather from the symbolic language of these two verses all that We have purposed to propound, and thus to attain, through the grace of the All-Merciful, the resplendent morn of certitude. Such are the strains of celestial melody which the immortal Bird of Heaven, warbling upon the Sadrih of Bahá, poureth out upon thee, that, by the permission of God, thou mayest tread the path of divine knowledge and wisdom.

And now, concerning His words: "And He shall send His angels. . . ." By "angels" is meant those who, reinforced by the power of the spirit, have

[1] Qur'án 3:119.

consumed, with the fire of the love of God, all human traits and limitations, and have clothed themselves with the attributes of the most exalted Beings and of the Cherubim. That holy man, Ṣádiq,[1] in his eulogy of the Cherubim, saith: "There stand a company of our fellow-Shí'ihs behind the Throne." Divers and manifold are the interpretations of the words "behind the Throne." In one sense, they indicate that no true Shí'ihs exist. Even as he hath said in another passage: "A true believer is likened unto the philosopher's stone." Addressing subsequently his listener, he saith: "Hast thou ever seen the philosopher's stone?" Reflect, how this symbolic language, more eloquent than any speech, however direct, testifieth to the non-existence of a true believer. Such is the testimony of Ṣádiq. And now consider, how unfair and numerous are those who, although they themselves have failed to inhale the fragrance of belief, have condemned as infidels those by whose word belief itself is recognized and established.

And now, inasmuch as these holy beings have sanctified themselves from every human limitation, have become endowed with the attributes of the

[1] The sixth Imám of the Shí'ihs.

spiritual, and have been adorned with the noble traits of the blessed, they therefore have been designated as "angels." Such is the meaning of these verses, every word of which hath been expounded by the aid of the most lucid texts, the most convincing arguments, and the best established evidences.

As the adherents of Jesus have never understood the hidden meaning of these words, and as the signs which they and the leaders of their Faith have expected have failed to appear, they therefore refused to acknowledge, even until now, the truth of those Manifestations of Holiness that have since the days of Jesus been made manifest. They have thus deprived themselves of the outpourings of God's holy grace, and of the wonders of His divine utterance. Such is their low estate in this, the Day of Resurrection! They have even failed to perceive that were the signs of the Manifestation of God in every age to appear in the visible realm in accordance with the text of established traditions, none could possibly deny or turn away, nor would the blessed be distinguished from the miserable, and the transgressor from the God-fearing. Judge fairly: Were the prophecies recorded in the

Gospel to be literally fulfilled; were Jesus, Son of Mary, accompanied by angels, to descend from the visible heaven upon the clouds; who would dare to disbelieve, who would dare to reject the truth, and wax disdainful? Nay, such consternation would immediately seize all the dwellers of the earth that no soul would feel able to utter a word, much less to reject or accept the truth. It was owing to their misunderstanding of these truths that many a Christian divine hath objected to Muḥammad, and voiced his protest in such words: "If Thou art in truth the promised Prophet, why then art Thou not accompanied by those angels our sacred Books foretold, and which must needs descend with the promised Beauty to assist Him in His Revelation and act as warners unto His people?" Even as the All-Glorious hath recorded their statement: "Why hath not an angel been sent down to him, so that he should have been a warner with Him?" [1]

Such objections and differences have persisted in every age and century. The people have always busied themselves with such specious discourses, vainly protesting: "Wherefore hath not this or that sign appeared?" Such ills befell them only because

[1] Qur'án 25:7.

they have clung to the ways of the divines of the age in which they lived, and blindly imitated them in accepting or denying these Essences of Detachment, these holy and divine Beings. These leaders, owing to their immersion in selfish desires, and their pursuit of transitory and sordid things, have regarded these divine Luminaries as being opposed to the standards of their knowledge and understanding, and the opponents of their ways and judgments. As they have literally interpreted the Word of God, and the sayings and traditions of the Letters of Unity, and expounded them according to their own deficient understanding, they have therefore deprived themselves and all their people of the bountiful showers of the grace and mercies of God. And yet they bear witness to this well-known tradition: "Verily Our Word is abstruse, bewilderingly abstruse." In another instance, it is said: "Our Cause is sorely trying, highly perplexing; none can bear it except a favorite of heaven, or an inspired Prophet, or he whose faith God hath tested." These leaders of religion admit that none of these three specified conditions is applicable to them. The first two conditions are manifestly beyond their reach; as to the third, it is evident that at no time have they been proof against those tests that have been sent by God, and that when the divine Touchstone appeared, they have shown themselves to be naught but dross.

Great God! Notwithstanding their acceptance of the truth of this tradition, these divines who are still doubtful of, and dispute about, the theological obscurities of their faith, yet claim to be the exponents of the subtleties of the law of God, and the expounders of the essential mysteries of His holy Word. They confidently assert that such traditions as indicate the advent of the expected Qá'im have not yet been fulfilled, whilst they themselves have failed to inhale the fragrance of the meaning of these traditions, and are still oblivious of the fact that all the signs foretold have come to pass, that the way of God's holy Cause hath been revealed, and the concourse of the faithful, swift as lightning, are, even now, passing upon that way, whilst these foolish divines wait expecting to witness the signs foretold. Say, O ye foolish ones! Wait ye even as those before you are waiting!

Were they to be questioned concerning those signs that must needs herald the revelation and rise of the sun of the Muḥammadan Dispensation, to which We have already referred, none of which have been literally fulfilled, and were it to be said to them: "Wherefore have ye rejected the claims advanced by Christians and the peoples of other faiths and regard them as infidels," knowing not what answer to give, they will reply: "These Books have been corrupted and are not, and never have been, of God." Reflect: the words of the verses themselves eloquently testify to the truth that they are of God. A similar verse hath been also revealed in the Qur'án, were ye of them that comprehend. Verily I say, throughout all this period they have utterly failed to comprehend what is meant by corrupting the text.

Yea, in the writings and utterances of the Mirrors reflecting the sun of the Muḥammadan Dispensation mention hath been made of "Modification by the exalted beings" and "alteration by the disdainful." Such passages, however, refer only to particular cases. Among them is the story of Ibn-i-Ṣúríyá. When the people of Khaybar asked the focal center of the Muḥammadan Revelation concerning the penalty of adultery committed between a married man and a married woman, Muḥammad answered and said: "The law of God is death by stoning." Whereupon they protested saying:

"No such law hath been revealed in the Pentateuch." Muḥammad answered and said: "Whom do ye regard among your rabbis as being a recognized authority and having a sure knowledge of the truth?" They agreed upon Ibn-i-Ṣúríyá. Thereupon Muḥammad summoned him and said: "I adjure thee by God Who clove the sea for you, caused manna to descend upon you, and the cloud to overshadow you, Who delivered you from Pharaoh and his people, and exalted you above all human beings, to tell us what Moses hath decreed concerning adultery between a married man and a married woman." He made reply: "O Muḥammad! death by stoning is the law." Muḥammad observed: "Why is it then that this law is annulled and hath ceased to operate among the Jews?" He answered and said: "When Nebuchadnezzar delivered Jerusalem to the flames, and put the Jews to death, only a few survived. The divines of that age, considering the extremely limited number of the Jews, and the multitude of the Amalekites, took counsel together, and came to the conclusion that were they to enforce the law of the Pentateuch, every survivor who hath been delivered from the hand of Nebuchadnezzar would have to be put to death according to the verdict of the Book. Owing

[85]

to such considerations, they totally repealed the penalty of death." Meanwhile Gabriel inspired Muḥammad's illumined heart with these words: "They pervert the text of the Word of God." [1]

This is one of the instances that have been referred to. Verily by "perverting" the text is not meant that which these foolish and abject souls have fancied, even as some maintain that Jewish and Christian divines have effaced from the Book such verses as extol and magnify the countenance of Muḥammad, and instead thereof have inserted the contrary. How utterly vain and false are these words! Can a man who believeth in a book, and deemeth it to be inspired by God, mutilate it? Moreover, the Pentateuch had been spread over the surface of all the earth, and was not confined to Mecca and Medina, so that they could privily corrupt and pervert its text. Nay, rather, by corruption of the text is meant that in which all Muslim divines are engaged today, that is the interpretation of God's holy Book in accordance with their idle imaginings and vain desires. And as the Jews, in the time of Muḥammad, interpreted those verses of the Pentateuch, that referred to His Manifesta-

[1] Qur'án 4:45.

tion, after their own fancy, and refused to be satisfied with His holy utterance, the charge of "perverting" the text was therefore pronounced against them. Likewise, it is clear, how in this day, the people of the Qur'án have perverted the text of God's holy Book, concerning the signs of the expected Manifestation, and interpreted it according to their inclination and desires.

In yet another instance, He saith: "A part of them heard the Word of God, and then, after they had understood it, distorted it, and knew that they did so."[1] This verse, too, doth indicate that the meaning of the Word of God hath been perverted, not that the actual words have been effaced. To the truth of this testify they that are sound of mind.

Again in another instance, He saith: "Woe unto those who, with their own hands, transcribe the Book corruptly, and then say: 'This is from God,' that they may sell it for some mean price."[2] This verse was revealed with reference to the divines and leaders of the Jewish Faith. These divines, in order to please the rich, acquire worldly emoluments, and give vent to their envy and misbelief,

[1] Qur'án 2:75.
[2] Qur'án 2:79.

wrote a number of treatises, refuting the claims of Muḥammad, supporting their arguments with such evidences as it would be improper to mention, and claimed that these arguments were derived from the text of the Pentateuch.

The same may be witnessed today. Consider how abundant are the denunciations written by the foolish divines of this age against this most wondrous Cause! How vain their imaginings that these calumnies are in conformity with the verses of God's sacred Book, and in consonance with the utterances of men of discernment!

Our purpose in relating these things is to warn you that were they to maintain that those verses wherein the signs referred to in the Gospel are mentioned have been perverted, were they to reject them, and cling instead to other verses and traditions, you should know that their words were utter falsehood and sheer calumny. Yea "corruption" of the text, in the sense We have referred to, hath been actually effected in particular instances. A few of these We have mentioned, that it may become manifest to every discerning observer that unto a few untutored holy Men hath been given the mastery of human learning, so that the malevolent opposer may cease to contend that a certain verse doth indicate "corruption" of the text, and insinuate that We, through lack of knowledge, have made mention of such things. Moreover, most of the verses that indicate "corruption" of the text have been revealed with reference to the Jewish people, were ye to explore the isles of Qur'ánic Revelation.

We have also heard a number of the foolish of the earth assert that the genuine text of the heavenly Gospel doth not exist amongst the Christians, that it hath ascended unto heaven. How grievously they have erred! How oblivious of the fact that such a statement imputeth the gravest injustice and tyranny to a gracious and loving Providence! How could God, when once the Day-star of the beauty of Jesus had disappeared from the sight of His people, and ascended unto the fourth heaven, cause His holy Book, His most great testimony amongst His creatures, to disappear also? What would be left to that people to cling to from the setting of the day-star of Jesus until the rise of the sun of the Muḥammadan Dispensation? What law could be their stay and guide? How could such people be made the victims of the avenging wrath of God, the omnipotent Avenger? How could they be afflicted with the scourge of chastisement by the heavenly King? Above all, how could the flow of the grace of the All-Bountiful be stayed? How could the ocean of His tender mercies be stilled? We take refuge with God, from that which His creatures have fancied about Him! Exalted is He above their comprehension!

Dear friend! Now when the light of God's everlasting Morn is breaking; when the radiance of His holy words: "God is the light of the heavens and of the earth" [1] is shedding illumination upon all mankind; when the inviolability of His tabernacle is being proclaimed by His sacred utterance: "God hath willed to perfect His light;" [2] and the Hand of omnipotence, bearing His testimony: "In His grasp He holdeth the kingdom of all things," is being outstretched unto all the peoples and kindreds of the earth; it behooveth us to gird up the loins of endeavour, that haply, by the grace and bounty of God, we may enter the celestial City: "Verily, we are God's," and abide within the exalted habitation: "And unto Him we do return."

[1] Qur'án 24:35.
[2] Qur'án 9:33.

It is incumbent upon thee, by the permission of God, to cleanse the eye of thine heart from the things of the world, that thou mayest realize the infinitude of divine knowledge, and mayest behold Truth so clearly that thou wilt need no proof to demonstrate His reality, nor any evidence to bear witness unto His testimony.

O affectionate seeker! Shouldst thou soar in the holy realm of the spirit, thou wouldst recognize God manifest and exalted above all things, in such wise that thine eyes would behold none else but Him. "God was alone; there was none else besides Him." So lofty is this station that no testimony can bear it witness, neither evidence do justice to its truth. Wert thou to explore the sacred domain of truth, thou wilt find that all things are known only by the light of His recognition, that He hath ever been, and will continue for ever to be, known through Himself. And if thou dwellest in the land of testimony, content thyself with that which He, Himself, hath revealed: "Is it not enough for them that We have sent down unto Thee the Book?" [1] This is the testimony which He, Himself, hath ordained; greater proof than this

[1] Qur'án 29:51.

there is none, nor ever will be: "This proof is
His Word; His own Self, the testimony of His
truth."

And now, We beseech the people of the Bayán,
all the learned, the sages, the divines, and witnesses
amongst them, not to forget the wishes and admonitions revealed in their Book. Let them, at all
times, fix their gaze upon the essentials of His
Cause, lest when He, Who is the Quintessence of
truth, the inmost Reality of all things, the Source
of all light, is made manifest, they cling unto certain passages of the Book, and inflict upon Him
that which was inflicted in the Dispensation of the
Qur'án. For, verily, powerful is He, the King of
divine might, to extinguish with one letter of His
wondrous words, the breath of life in the whole of
the Bayán and the people thereof, and with one
letter bestow upon them a new and everlasting life,
and cause them to arise and speed out of the
sepulchres of their vain and selfish desires. Take
heed, and be watchful; and remember that all
things have their consummation in belief in Him,
in attainment unto His day, and in the realization
of His divine presence. "There is no piety in turning your faces toward the east or toward the west,

but he is pious who believeth in God and the Last Day."[1] Give ear, O people of the Bayán, unto the truth whereunto We have admonished you, that haply ye may seek the shelter of the shadow extended, in the Day of God, upon all mankind.

[1] Qur'án 2:176.

END OF PART ONE

PART TWO

Verily He Who is the Day-star of Truth and Revealer of the Supreme Being holdeth, for all time, undisputed sovereignty over all that is in heaven and on earth, though no man be found on earth to obey Him. He verily is independent of all earthly dominion, though He be utterly destitute. Thus We reveal unto thee the mysteries of the Cause of God, and bestow upon thee the gems of divine wisdom, that haply thou mayest soar on the wings of renunciation to those heights that are veiled from the eyes of men.

THE significance and essential purpose underlying these words is to reveal and demonstrate unto the pure in heart and the sanctified in spirit that they Who are the Luminaries of truth and the Mirrors reflecting the light of divine Unity, in whatever age and cycle they are sent down from their invisible habitations of ancient glory unto this world, to educate the souls of men and endue with grace all created things, are invariably endowed with an all-compelling power, and invested with invincible sovereignty. For these hidden Gems, these concealed and invisible Treasures, in themselves manifest and vindicate the reality of these holy words: "Verily God doeth whatsoever He willeth, and ordaineth whatsoever He pleaseth."

To every discerning and illumined heart it is evident that God, the unknowable Essence, the divine Being, is immensely exalted beyond every human attribute, such as corporeal existence, ascent and descent, egress and regress. Far be it from His glory that human tongue should adequately recount His praise, or that human heart comprehend His fathomless mystery. He is and hath ever been veiled in the ancient eternity of His Essence, and will remain in His Reality everlastingly hidden from the sight of men. "No vision taketh in Him, but He taketh in all vision; He is the Subtile, the All-Perceiving." [1] No tie of direct intercourse can possibly bind Him to His creatures. He standeth exalted beyond and above all separation and union, all proximity and remoteness. No sign can indicate His presence or His absence; inasmuch as by a word of His command all that are in heaven and on earth have come to exist, and by His wish, which is the Primal Will itself, all have stepped out of utter nothingness into the realm of being, the world of the visible.

Gracious God! How could there be conceived any existing relationship or possible connection

[1] Qur'án 6:103.

between His Word and they that are created of it? The verse: "God would have you beware of Himself"[1] unmistakably beareth witness to the reality of Our argument, and the words: "God was alone; there was none else besides Him" are a sure testimony of its truth. All the Prophets of God and their chosen Ones, all the divines, the sages, and the wise of every generation, unanimously recognize their inability to attain unto the comprehension of that Quintessence of all truth, and confess their incapacity to grasp Him, Who is the inmost Reality of all things.

The door of the knowledge of the Ancient of Days being thus closed in the face of all beings, the Source of infinite grace, according to His saying: "His grace hath transcended all things; My grace hath encompassed them all" hath caused those luminous Gems of Holiness to appear out of the realm of the spirit, in the noble form of the human temple, and be made manifest unto all men, that they may impart unto the world the mysteries of the unchangeable Being, and tell of the subtleties of His imperishable Essence. These sanctified Mirrors, these Day-springs of ancient glory are one and all the Exponents on earth of Him Who is the

[1] Qur'án 3:28.

central Orb of the universe, its Essence and ultimate Purpose. From Him proceed their knowledge and power; from Him is derived their sovereignty. The beauty of their countenance is but a reflection of His image, and their revelation a sign of His deathless glory. They are the Treasuries of divine knowledge, and the Repositories of celestial wisdom. Through them is transmitted a grace that is infinite, and by them is revealed the light that can never fade. Even as He hath said: "There is no distinction whatsoever between Thee and them; except that they are Thy servants, and are created of Thee." This is the significance of the tradition: "I am He, Himself, and He is I, myself."

The traditions and sayings that bear direct reference to Our theme are divers and manifold; We have refrained from quoting them for the sake of brevity. Nay, whatever is in the heavens and whatever is on the earth is a direct evidence of the revelation within it of the attributes and names of God, inasmuch as within every atom are enshrined the signs that bear eloquent testimony to the revelation of that most great Light. Methinks, but for the potency of that revelation, no being could ever exist. How resplendent the luminaries of knowledge that shine in an atom, and how vast the oceans of wisdom that surge within a drop! To a supreme degree is this true of man, who, among all created things, hath been invested with the robe of such gifts, and hath been singled out for the glory of such distinction. For in him are potentially revealed all the attributes and names of God to a degree that no other created being hath excelled or surpassed. All these names and attributes are applicable to him. Even as He hath said: "Man is My mystery, and I am his mystery." Manifold are the verses that have been repeatedly revealed in all the heavenly Books and the holy Scriptures, expressive of this most subtle and lofty theme. Even as He hath revealed: "We will surely show them Our signs in the world and within themselves." [1] Again He saith: "And also in your own selves: will ye not then behold the signs of God?" [2] And yet again He revealeth: "And be ye not like those who forget God, and whom He hath therefore caused to forget their own selves." [3] In this connection, He Who is the eternal King—may the souls of all that dwell within the mystic Tabernacle be

[1] Qur'án 41:53.
[2] Qur'án 51:21.
[3] Qur'án 59:19.

a sacrifice unto Him—hath spoken: "He hath known God who hath known himself."

I swear by God, O esteemed and honoured friend! Shouldst thou ponder these words in thine heart, thou wilt of a certainty find the doors of divine wisdom and infinite knowledge flung open before thy face.

From that which hath been said it becometh evident that all things, in their inmost reality, testify to the revelation of the names and attributes of God within them. Each according to its capacity, indicateth, and is expressive of, the knowledge of God. So potent and universal is this revelation, that it hath encompassed all things, visible and invisible. Thus hath He revealed: "Hath aught else save Thee a power of revelation which is not possessed by Thee, that it could have manifested Thee? Blind is the eye which doth not perceive Thee." Likewise, hath the eternal King spoken: "No thing have I perceived, except that I perceived God within it, God before it, or God after it." Also in the tradition of Kumayl it is written: "Behold, a light hath shone forth out of the Morn of eternity, and lo! its waves have penetrated the inmost reality of all men." Man, the noblest and most perfect of all created things, excelleth them all in the intensity of this revelation, and is a fuller expression of its glory. And of all men, the most accomplished, the most distinguished and the most excellent are the Manifestations of the Sun of Truth. Nay, all else besides these Manifestations, live by the operation of their Will, and move and have their being through the outpourings of their grace. "But for Thee, I would have not created the heavens." Nay, all in their holy presence fade into utter nothingness, and are a thing forgotten. Human tongue can never befittingly sing their praise, and human speech can never unfold their mystery. These Tabernacles of holiness, these primal Mirrors which reflect the light of unfading glory, are but expressions of Him Who is the Invisible of the Invisibles. By the revelation of these gems of divine virtue all the names and attributes of God, such as knowledge and power, sovereignty and dominion, mercy and wisdom, glory, bounty and grace, are made manifest.

These attributes of God are not and have never been vouchsafed specially unto certain Prophets, and withheld from others. Nay, all the Prophets of God, His well-favoured, His holy, and chosen

Messengers, are, without exception, the bearers of His names, and the embodiments of His attributes. They only differ in the intensity of their revelation, and the comparative potency of their light. Even as He hath revealed: "Some of the Apostles We have caused to excel the others." [1] It hath therefore become manifest and evident that within the tabernacles of these Prophets and chosen Ones of God the light of His infinite names and exalted attributes hath been reflected, even though the light of some of these attributes may or may not be outwardly revealed from these luminous Temples to the eyes of men. That a certain attribute of God hath not been outwardly manifested by these Essences of Detachment doth in no wise imply that they Who are the Daysprings of God's attributes and the Treasuries of His holy names did not actually possess it. Therefore, these illuminated Souls, these beauteous Countenances have, each and every one of them, been endowed with all the attributes of God, such as sovereignty, dominion, and the like, even though to outward seeming they be shorn of all earthly majesty. To every discerning eye this is evident and manifest; it requireth neither proof nor evidence.

[1] Qur'án 2:253.

Yea, inasmuch as the peoples of the world have failed to seek from the luminous and crystal Springs of divine knowledge the inner meaning of God's holy words, they therefore have languished, stricken and sore athirst, in the vale of idle fancy and waywardness. They have strayed far from the fresh and thirst-subduing waters, and gathered round the salt that burneth bitterly. Concerning them, the Dove of Eternity hath spoken: "And if they see the path of righteousness, they will not take it for their path; but if they see the path of error, for their path will they take it. This, because they treated Our signs as lies, and were heedless of them." [1]

To this testifieth that which hath been witnessed in this wondrous and exalted Dispensation. Myriads of holy verses have descended from the heaven of might and grace, yet no one hath turned thereunto, nor ceased to cling to those words of men, not one letter of which they that have spoken them comprehend. For this reason the people have doubted incontestable truths, such as these, and caused themselves to be deprived of the Riḍván of

[1] Qur'án 7:145.

divine knowledge, and the eternal meads of celestial wisdom.

And now, to resume Our argument concerning the question: Why is it that the sovereignty of the Qá'im, affirmed in the text of recorded traditions, and handed down by the shining stars of the Muḥammadan Dispensation, hath not in the least been made manifest? Nay, the contrary hath come to pass. Have not His disciples and companions been afflicted of men? Are they not still the victims of the fierce opposition of their enemies? Are they not today leading the life of abased and impotent mortals? Yea, the sovereignty attributed to the Qá'im and spoken of in the scriptures, is a reality, the truth of which none can doubt. This sovereignty, however, is not the sovereignty which the minds of men have falsely imagined. Moreover, the Prophets of old, each and every one, whenever announcing to the people of their day the advent of the coming Revelation, have invariably and specifically referred to that sovereignty with which the promised Manifestation must needs be invested. This is attested by the records of the scriptures of the past. This sovereignty hath not been solely and exclusively at-

tributed to the Qá'im. Nay rather, the attribute of
sovereignty and all other names and attributes of
God have been and will ever be vouchsafed unto
all the Manifestations of God, before and after
Him, inasmuch as these Manifestations, as it hath
already been explained, are the Embodiments of
the attributes of God, the Invisible, and the Revealers of the divine mysteries.

Furthermore, by sovereignty is meant the all-
encompassing, all-pervading power which is in-
herently exercised by the Qá'im whether or not He
appear to the world clothed in the majesty of
earthly dominion. This is solely dependent upon
the will and pleasure of the Qá'im Himself. You
will readily recognize that the terms sovereignty,
wealth, life, death, judgment and resurrection,
spoken of by the scriptures of old, are not what
this generation hath conceived and vainly imagined. Nay, by sovereignty is meant that sovereignty
which in every dispensation resideth within, and
is exercised by, the person of the Manifestation,
the Day-star of Truth. That sovereignty is the spiritual ascendancy which He exerciseth to the fullest
degree over all that is in heaven and on earth, and
which in due time revealeth itself to the world in

direct proportion to its capacity and spiritual receptiveness, even as the sovereignty of Muḥammad, the Messenger of God, is today apparent
and manifest amongst the people. You are well
aware of what befell His Faith in the early days
of His dispensation. What woeful sufferings did
the hand of the infidel and erring, the divines of
that age and their associates, inflict upon that spiritual Essence, that most pure and holy Being! How
abundant the thorns and briars which they have
strewn over His path! It is evident that wretched
generation, in their wicked and satanic fancy, regarded every injury to that immortal Being as a
means to the attainment of an abiding felicity;
inasmuch as the recognized divines of that age,
such as 'Abdu'lláh-i-Ubayy, Abú-'Ámir, the hermit,
Ka'b-Ibn-i-Ashraf, and Naḍr-Ibn-i-Ḥárith, all
treated Him as an impostor, and pronounced Him
a lunatic and a calumniator. Such sore accusations
they brought against Him that in recounting them
God forbiddeth the ink to flow, Our pen to move,
or the page to bear them. These malicious imputations provoked the people to arise and torment
Him. And how fierce that torment if the divines
of the age be its chief instigators, if they denounce
Him to their followers, cast Him out from their

midst, and declare Him a miscreant! Hath not the same befallen this Servant, and been witnessed by all?

For this reason did Muḥammad cry out: "No Prophet of God hath suffered such harm as I have suffered." And in the Qur'án are recorded all the calumnies and reproaches uttered against Him, as well as all the afflictions which He suffered. Refer ye thereunto, that haply ye may be informed of that which hath befallen His Revelation. So grievous was His plight, that for a time all ceased to hold intercourse with Him and His companions. Whoever associated with Him fell a victim to the relentless cruelty of His enemies.

We shall cite in this connection only one verse of that Book. Shouldst thou observe it with a discerning eye, thou wilt, all the remaining days of thy life, lament and bewail the injury of Muḥammad, that wronged and oppressed Messenger of God. That verse was revealed at a time when Muḥammad languished weary and sorrowful beneath the weight of the opposition of the people, and of their unceasing torture. In the midst of His agony, the Voice of Gabriel, calling from the Sadratu'l-Muntahá, was heard saying: "But if their opposition be grievous to Thee—if Thou canst, seek out an opening into the earth or a ladder into heaven."[1] The implication of this utterance is that His case had no remedy, that they would not withhold their hands from Him unless He should hide Himself beneath the depths of the earth, or take His flight unto heaven.

Consider, how great is the change today! Behold, how many are the Sovereigns who bow the knee before His name! How numerous the nations and kingdoms who have sought the shelter of His shadow, who bear allegiance to His Faith, and pride themselves therein! From the pulpit-top there ascendeth today the words of praise which, in utter lowliness, glorify His blessed name; and from the heights of minarets there resoundeth the call that summoneth the concourse of His people to adore Him. Even those Kings of the earth who have refused to embrace His Faith and to put off the garment of unbelief, none the less confess and acknowledge the greatness and overpowering majesty of that Day-star of loving kindness. Such is His earthly sovereignty, the evidences of which thou dost on every side behold. This sovereignty

[1] Qur'án 6:35.

must needs be revealed and established either in the lifetime of every Manifestation of God or after His ascension unto His true habitation in the realms above. What thou dost witness today is but a confirmation of this truth. That spiritual ascendancy, however, which is primarily intended, resideth within, and revolveth around Them from eternity even unto eternity. It can never for a moment be divorced from Them. Its dominion hath encompassed all that is in heaven and on earth.

The following is an evidence of the sovereignty exercised by Muḥammad, the Day-star of Truth. Hast thou not heard how with one single verse He hath sundered light from darkness, the righteous from the ungodly, and the believing from the infidel? All the signs and allusions concerning the Day of Judgment, which thou hast heard, such as the raising of the dead, the Day of Reckoning, the Last Judgment, and others have been made manifest through the revelation of that verse. These revealed words were a blessing to the righteous who on hearing them exclaimed: "O God our Lord, we have heard, and obeyed." They were a curse to the people of iniquity who, on hearing them affirmed: "We have heard and rebelled." Those

words, sharp as the sword of God, have separated
the faithful from the infidel, and severed father
from son. Thou hast surely witnessed how they
that have confessed their faith in Him and they
that rejected Him have warred against each other,
and sought one another's property. How many
fathers have turned away from their sons; how
many lovers have shunned their beloved! So merci-
lessly trenchant was this wondrous sword of God
that it cleft asunder every relationship! On the
other hand, consider the welding power of His
Word. Observe, how those in whose midst the
Satan of self had for years sown the seeds of malice
and hate became so fused and blended through
their allegiance to this wondrous and transcendent
Revelation that it seemed as if they had sprung
from the same loins. Such is the binding force of
the Word of God, which uniteth the hearts of them
that have renounced all else but Him, who have
believed in His signs, and quaffed from the Hand
of glory the Kawthar of God's holy grace. Furthermore, how numerous are those peoples of divers beliefs, of conflicting creeds, and opposing tem-
peraments, who, through the reviving fragrance of
the Divine springtime, breathing from the Riḍván
of God, have been arrayed with the new robe of

divine Unity, and have drunk from the cup of His singleness!

This is the significance of the well-known words: "The wolf and the lamb shall feed together." [1] Behold the ignorance and folly of those who, like the nations of old, are still expecting to witness the time when these beasts will feed together in one pasture! Such is their low estate. Methinks, never have their lips touched the cup of understanding, neither have their feet trodden the path of justice. Besides, of what profit would it be to the world were such a thing to take place? How well hath He spoken concerning them: "Hearts have they, with which they understand not, and eyes have they with which they see not!" [2]

Consider how with this one verse which hath descended from the heaven of the Will of God, the world and all that is therein have been brought to a reckoning with Him. Whosoever acknowledged His truth and turned unto Him, his good works outweighed his misdeeds, and all his sins were remitted and forgiven. Thereby is the truth of these words concerning Him made manifest: "Swift is

[1] Isaiah 65:25.
[2] Qur'án 7:178.

He in reckoning." Thus God turneth iniquity into righteousness, were ye to explore the realms of divine knowledge, and fathom the mysteries of His wisdom. In like manner, whosoever partook of the cup of love, obtained his portion of the ocean of eternal grace and of the showers of everlasting mercy, and entered into the life of faith—the heavenly and everlasting life. But he that turned away from that cup was condemned to eternal death. By the terms "life" and "death," spoken of in the scriptures, is intended the life of faith and the death of unbelief. The generality of the people, owing to their failure to grasp the meaning of these words, rejected and despised the person of the Manifestation, deprived themselves of the light of His divine guidance, and refused to follow the example of that immortal Beauty.

When the light of Qur'ánic Revelation was kindled within the chamber of Muḥammad's holy heart, He passed upon the people the verdict of the Last Day, the verdict of resurrection, of judgment, of life, and of death. Thereupon the standards of revolt were hoisted, and the doors of derision opened. Thus hath He, the Spirit of God, recorded, as spoken by the infidels: "And if thou shouldst say, 'After death ye shall surely be raised again,' the infidels will certainly exclaim, 'This is nothing but manifest sorcery.' " [1] Again He speaketh: "If ever thou dost marvel, marvellous surely is their saying, 'What! When we have become dust, shall we be restored in a new creation?' " [2] Thus, in another passage, He wrathfully exclaimeth: "Are We wearied out with the first creation? Yet are they in doubt with regard to a new creation!" [3]

As the commentators of the Qur'án and they that follow the letter thereof misapprehended the inner meaning of the words of God and failed to grasp their essential purpose, they sought to demonstrate that, according to the rules of grammar, whenever the term "idhá" (meaning "if" or "when") precedeth the past tense, it invariably hath reference to the future. Later, they were sore perplexed in attempting to explain those verses of the Book wherein that term did not actually occur. Even as He hath revealed: "And there was a blast on the trumpet,—lo! it is the threatened Day! And every soul is summoned to a reckoning,—with

[1] Qur'án 11:7.
[2] Qur'án 13:5.
[3] Qur'án 50:15.

him an impeller and a witness."[1] In explaining this and similar verses, they have in some cases argued that the term "idhá" is implied. In other instances, they have idly contended that whereas the Day of Judgment is inevitable, it hath therefore been referred to as an event not of the future but of the past. How vain their sophistry! How grievous their blindness! They refuse to recognize the trumpet-blast which so explicitly in this text was sounded through the revelation of Muḥammad. They deprive themselves of the regenerating Spirit of God that breathed into it, and foolishly expect to hear the trumpet-sound of the Seraph of God who is but one of His servants! Hath not the Seraph himself, the angel of the Judgment Day, and his like been ordained by Muḥammad's own utterance? Say: What! Will ye give that which is for your good in exchange for that which is evil? Wretched is that which ye have falsely exchanged! Surely ye are a people, evil, in grievous loss.

Nay, by "trumpet" is meant the trumpet-call of Muḥammad's Revelation, which was sounded in the heart of the universe, and by "resurrection" is meant His own rise to proclaim the Cause of God.

[1] Qur'án 50:20.

He bade the erring and wayward arise and speed out of the sepulchres of their bodies, arrayed them with the beauteous robe of faith, and quickened them with the breath of a new and wondrous life. Thus at the hour when Muḥammad, that divine Beauty, purposed to unveil one of the mysteries hidden in the symbolic terms "resurrection," "judgment," "paradise," and "hell," Gabriel, the Voice of Inspiration, was heard saying: "Erelong will they wag their heads at Thee, and say, 'When shall this be?' Say: 'Perchance it is nigh.' " [1] The implications of this verse alone suffice the peoples of the world, were they to ponder it in their hearts.

Gracious God! How far have that people strayed from the way of God! Although the Day of Resurrection was ushered in through the Revelation of Muḥammad, although His light and tokens had encompassed the earth and all that is therein, yet that people derided Him, gave themselves up to those idols which the divines of that age, in their vain and idle fancy, had conceived, and deprived themselves of the light of heavenly grace and of the showers of divine mercy. Yea, the abject beetle can never scent the fragrance of holiness, and the

[1] Qur'án 17:51.

bat of darkness can never face the splendour of the sun.

Such things have come to pass in the days of every Manifestation of God. Even as Jesus said: "Ye must be born again." [1] Again He saith: "Except a man be born of water and of the Spirit, he cannot enter into the Kingdom of God. That which is born of the flesh is flesh; and that which is born of the Spirit is spirit." [2] The purport of these words is that whosoever in every dispensation is born of the Spirit and is quickened by the breath of the Manifestation of Holiness, he verily is of those that have attained unto "life" and "resurrection" and have entered into the "paradise" of the love of God. And whosoever is not of them, is condemned to "death" and "deprivation," to the "fire" of unbelief, and to the "wrath" of God. In all the scriptures, the books and chronicles, the sentence of death, of fire, of blindness, of want of understanding and hearing, hath been pronounced against those whose lips have tasted not the ethereal cup of true knowledge, and whose hearts have been deprived of the grace of the holy Spirit in their day.

[1] John 3:7.
[2] John 3:5-6.

Even as it hath been previously recorded: "Hearts have they with which they understand not."[1]

In another passage of the Gospel it is written: "And it came to pass that on a certain day the father of one of the disciples of Jesus had died. That disciple reporting the death of his father unto Jesus, asked for leave to go and bury him. Whereupon, Jesus, that Essence of Detachment, answered and said: "Let the dead bury their dead."[2]

In like manner, two of the people of Kúfih went to 'Alí, the Commander of the Faithful. One owned a house and wished to sell it; the other was to be the purchaser. They had agreed that this transaction should be effected and the contract be written with the knowledge of 'Alí. He, the exponent of the law of God, addressing the scribe, said: "Write thou: 'A dead man hath bought from another dead man a house. That house is bounded by four limits. One extendeth toward the tomb, the other to the vault of the grave, the third to the Ṣiráṭ, the fourth to either Paradise or hell.' " Reflect, had these two souls been quickened by the trumpet-call of 'Alí, had they risen from the grave

[1] Qur'án 7:178.
[2] Luke 9:60.

of error by the power of his love, the judgment of death would certainly not have been pronounced against them.

In every age and century, the purpose of the Prophets of God and their chosen ones hath been no other but to affirm the spiritual significance of the terms "life," "resurrection," and "judgment." If one will ponder but for a while this utterance of 'Alí in his heart, one will surely discover all mysteries hidden in the terms "grave," "tomb," "ṣiráṭ," "paradise" and "hell." But oh! how strange and pitiful! Behold, all the people are imprisoned within the tomb of self, and lie buried beneath the nethermost depths of worldly desire! Wert thou to attain to but a dewdrop of the crystal waters of divine knowledge, thou wouldst readily realize that true life is not the life of the flesh but the life of the spirit. For the life of the flesh is common to both men and animals, whereas the life of the spirit is possessed only by the pure in heart who have quaffed from the ocean of faith and partaken of the fruit of certitude. This life knoweth no death, and this existence is crowned by immortality. Even as it hath been said: "He who is a true believer liveth both in this world and in the world to come."

If by "life" be meant this earthly life, it is evident that death must needs overtake it.

Similarly, the records of all the scriptures bear witness to this lofty truth and this most exalted word. Moreover, this verse of the Qur'án, revealed concerning Ḥamzih, the "Prince of Martyrs,"[1] and Abú-Jahl, is a luminous evidence and sure testimony of the truth of Our saying: "Shall the dead, whom We have quickened, and for whom We have ordained a light whereby he may walk among men, be like him, whose likeness is in the darkness, whence he will not come forth?"[2] This verse descended from the heaven of the Primal Will at a time when Ḥamzih had already been invested with the sacred mantle of faith, and Abú-Jahl had waxed relentless in his opposition and unbelief. From the Wellspring of omnipotence and the Source of eternal holiness, there came the judgment that conferred everlasting life upon Ḥamzih, and condemned Abú-Jahl to eternal damnation. This was the signal that caused the fires of unbelief to glow with the hottest flame in the heart of the infidels, and provoked them openly to repudi-

---

[1] Title of the uncle of Muḥammad.
[2] Qur'án 6:122.

ate His truth. They loudly clamoured: "When did
Ḥamzih die? When was he risen? At what hour
was such a life conferred upon him?" As they understood not the significance of these noble sayings,
nor sought enlightenment from the recognized expounders of the Faith, that these might confer a
sprinkling of the Kawthar of divine knowledge
upon them, therefore such fires of mischief were
kindled amongst men.

Thou dost witness today how, notwithstanding
the radiant splendour of the Sun of divine knowledge, all the people, whether high or low, have
clung to the ways of those abject manifestations of
the Prince of Darkness. They continually appeal
to them for aid in unraveling the intricacies of
their Faith, and, owing to lack of knowledge, they
make such replies as can in no wise damage their
fame and fortune. It is evident that these souls, vile
and miserable as the beetle itself, have had no portion of the musk-laden breeze of eternity, and have
never entered the Riḍván of heavenly delight.
How, therefore, can they impart unto others the
imperishable fragrance of holiness? Such is their
way, and such will it remain for ever. Only those
will attain to the knowledge of the Word of God

that have turned unto Him, and repudiated the manifestations of Satan. Thus God hath reaffirmed the law of the day of His Revelation, and inscribed it with the pen of power upon the mystic Tablet hidden beneath the veil of celestial glory. Wert thou to heed these words, wert thou to ponder their outward and inner meaning in thy heart, thou wouldst seize the significance of all the abstruse problems which, in this day, have become insuperable barriers between men and the knowledge of the Day of Judgment. Then wilt thou have no more questions to perplex thee. We fain would hope that, God willing, thou wilt not return, deprived and still athirst, from the shores of the ocean of divine mercy, nor come back destitute from the imperishable Sanctuary of thy heart's desire. Let it now be seen what thy search and endeavours will achieve.

To resume: Our purpose in setting forth these truths hath been to demonstrate the sovereignty of Him Who is the King of kings. Be fair: Is this sovereignty which, through the utterance of one Word, hath manifested such pervading influence, ascendancy, and awful majesty, is this sovereignty superior, or is the worldly dominion of these kings of the earth who, despite their solicitude for their subjects and their help of the poor, are assured only of an outward and fleeting allegiance, while in the hearts of men they inspire neither affection nor respect? Hath not that sovereignty, through the potency of one word, subdued, quickened, and revitalized the whole world? What! Can the lowly dust compare with Him Who is the Lord of Lords? What tongue dare utter the immensity of difference that lieth between them? Nay, all comparison falleth short in attaining the hallowed sanctuary of His sovereignty. Were man to reflect, he would surely perceive that even the servant of His threshold ruleth over all created things! This hath already been witnessed, and will in future be made manifest.

This is but one of the meanings of the spiritual sovereignty which We have set forth in accordance with the capacity and receptiveness of the people. For He, the Mover of all beings, that glorified Countenance, is the source of such potencies as neither this wronged One can reveal, nor this unworthy people comprehend. Immensely exalted is He above men's praise of His sovereignty; glorified is He beyond that which they attribute unto Him!

And now, ponder this in thine heart: Were sovereignty to mean earthly sovereignty and worldly dominion, were it to imply the subjection and external allegiance of all the peoples and kindreds of the earth—whereby His loved ones should be exalted and be made to live in peace, and His enemies be abased and tormented—such form of sovereignty would not be true of God Himself, the Source of all dominion, Whose majesty and power all things testify. For, dost thou not witness how the generality of mankind is under the sway of His enemies? Have they not all turned away from the path of His good-pleasure? Have they not done that which He hath forbidden, and left undone, nay repudiated and opposed, those things which He hath commanded? Have not His friends ever been the victims of the tyranny of His foes? All these things are more obvious than even the splendour of the noon-tide sun.

Know, therefore, O questioning seeker, that earthly sovereignty is of no worth, nor will it ever be, in the eyes of God and His chosen Ones. Moreover, if ascendancy and dominion be interpreted to mean earthly supremacy and temporal power, how impossible will it be for thee to explain these

verses: "And verily Our host shall conquer." [1]
"Fain would they put out God's light with their
mouths: But God hath willed to perfect His light,
albeit the infidels abhor it." [2] "He is the Dominant,
above all things." Similarly, most of the Qur'án
testifieth to this truth.

Were the idle contention of these foolish and
despicable souls to be true, they would have none
other alternative than to reject all these holy
utterances and heavenly allusions. For no warrior
could be found on earth more excellent and nearer
to God than Ḥusayn, son of 'Alí, so peerless and
incomparable was he. "There was none to equal or
to match him in the world." Yet, thou must have
heard what befell him. "God's malison on the head
of the people of tyranny!" [3]

Were the verse "And verily Our host shall conquer" to be literally interpreted, it is evident that
it would in no wise be applicable to the chosen
Ones of God and His hosts, inasmuch as Ḥusayn,
whose heroism was manifest as the sun, crushed
and subjugated, quaffed at last the cup of martyrdom in Karbilá, the land of Ṭaff. Similarly, the

[1] Qur'án 37:173.
[2] Qur'án 9:33.
[3] Qur'án 11:18.

sacred verse "Fain would they put out God's light with their mouths: But God hath willed to perfect His light, albeit the infidels abhor it." Were it to be literally interpreted it would never correspond with the truth. For in every age the light of God hath, to outward seeming, been quenched by the peoples of the earth, and the Lamps of God extinguished by them. How then could the ascendancy of the sovereignty of these Lamps be explained? What could the potency of God's will to "perfect His light" signify? As hath already been witnessed, so great was the enmity of the infidels, that none of these divine Luminaries ever found a place for shelter, or tasted of the cup of tranquillity. So heavily were they oppressed, that the least of men inflicted upon these Essences of being whatsoever he listed. These sufferings have been observed and measured by the people. How, therefore, can such people be capable of understanding and expounding these words of God, these verses of everlasting glory?

But the purpose of these verses is not what they have imagined. Nay, the terms "ascendancy," "power," and "authority" imply a totally different station and meaning. For instance, consider the pervading power of those drops of the blood of Ḥusayn which besprinkled the earth. What ascendancy and influence hath the dust itself, through the sacredness and potency of that blood, exercised over the bodies and souls of men! So much so, that he who sought deliverance from his ills, was healed by touching the dust of that holy ground, and whosoever, wishing to protect his property, treasured with absolute faith and understanding, a little of that holy earth within his house, safeguarded all his possessions. These are the outward manifestations of its potency. And were We to recount its hidden virtues they would assuredly say: "He verily hath considered the dust to be the Lord of Lords, and hath utterly forsaken the Faith of God."

Furthermore, call to mind the shameful circumstances that have attended the martyrdom of Ḥusayn. Reflect upon his loneliness, how, to outer seeming, none could be found to aid him, none to take up his body and bury it. And yet, behold how numerous, in this day, are those who from the uttermost corners of the earth don the garb of pilgrimage, seeking the site of his martyrdom, that there they may lay their heads upon the threshold of his shrine! Such is the ascendancy and power of God! Such is the glory of His dominion and majesty!

Think not that because these things have come to pass after Ḥusayn's martyrdom, therefore all this glory hath been of no profit unto him. For that holy soul is immortal, liveth the life of God, and abideth within the retreats of celestial glory upon the Sadrih of heavenly reunion. These Essences of being are the shining Exemplars of sacrifice. They have offered, and will continue to offer up their lives, their substance, their souls, their spirit, their all, in the path of the Well-Beloved. By them, no station, however exalted, could be more dearly cherished. For lovers have no desire but the good-pleasure of their Beloved, and have no aim except reunion with Him.

Should We wish to impart unto thee a glimmer of the mysteries of Ḥusayn's martyrdom, and reveal unto thee the fruits thereof, these pages could never suffice, nor exhaust their meaning. Our hope is that, God willing, the breeze of mercy may blow, and the divine Springtime clothe the tree of being with the robe of a new life; so that we may discover the mysteries of divine Wisdom, and, through His providence, be made independent of the knowledge of all things. We have, as yet, descried none but a handful of souls, destitute of all renown, who have attained unto this station. Let the future disclose what the Judgment of God will ordain, and the Tabernacle of His decree reveal. In such wise We recount unto thee the wonders of the Cause of God, and pour out into thine ears the strains of heavenly melody, that haply thou mayest attain unto the station of true knowledge, and partake of the fruit thereof. Therefore, know thou of a certainty that these Luminaries of heavenly majesty, though their dwelling be in the dust, yet their true habitation is the seat of glory in the realms above. Though bereft of all earthly possessions, yet they soar in the realms of immeasurable riches. And whilst sore tried in the grip of the enemy, they are seated on the right hand of power and celestial dominion. Amidst the darkness of their abasement there shineth upon them the light of unfading glory, and upon their helplessness are showered the tokens of an invincible sovereignty.

Thus Jesus, Son of Mary, whilst seated one day and speaking in the strain of the Holy Spirit, uttered words such as these: "O people! My food is the grass of the field, wherewith I satisfy my hunger. My bed is the dust, my lamp in the night the light of the moon, and my steed my own feet. Behold, who on earth is richer than I?" By the righteousness of God! Thousands of treasures circle round this poverty, and a myriad kingdoms of glory yearn for such abasement! Shouldst thou attain to a drop of the ocean of the inner meaning of these words, thou wouldst surely forsake the world and all that is therein, and, as the Phoenix wouldst consume thyself in the flames of the undying Fire.

In like manner, it is related that on a certain day, one of the companions of Ṣádiq complained of his poverty before him. Whereupon, Ṣádiq, that immortal beauty, made reply: "Verily thou art rich, and hast drunk the draught of wealth." That poverty-stricken soul was perplexed at the words uttered by that luminous countenance, and said: "Where are my riches, I who stand in need of a single coin?" Ṣádiq thereupon observed: "Dost thou not possess our love?" He replied: "Yea, I possess it, O thou scion of the Prophet of God!" And Ṣádiq asked him saying: "Exchangest thou this love for one thousand dinars?" He answered: "Nay, never will I exchange it, though the world and all that is therein be given me!" Then Ṣádiq remarked: "How can he who possesses such a treasure be called poor?"

This poverty and these riches, this abasement and glory, this dominion, power, and the like, upon which the eyes and hearts of these vain and foolish souls are set,—all these things fade into utter nothingness in that Court! Even as He hath said: "O men! Ye are but paupers in need of God; but God is the Rich, the Self-Sufficing." [1] By 'riches' therefore is meant independence of all else but God, and by 'poverty' the lack of things that are of God.

Similarly, call thou to mind the day when the Jews, who had surrounded Jesus, Son of Mary, were pressing Him to confess His claim of being the Messiah and Prophet of God, so that they might declare Him an infidel and sentence Him to death. Then, they led Him away, He Who was the Day-star of the heaven of divine Revelation, unto Pilate and Caiaphas, who was the leading divine of that age. The chief priests were all assembled in the palace, also a multitude of people who had gathered to witness His sufferings, to deride and injure Him. Though they repeatedly ques-

[1] Qur'án 35:15.

tioned Him, hoping that He would confess His claim, yet Jesus held His peace and spake not. Finally, an accursed of God arose and, approaching Jesus, adjured Him saying: "Didst thou not claim to be the Divine Messiah? Didst thou not say, 'I am the King of Kings, My word is the Word of God, and I am the breaker of the Sabbath day?'" Thereupon Jesus lifted up His head and said: "Beholdest thou not the Son of Man sitting on the right hand of power and might?" These were His words, and yet consider how to outward seeming He was devoid of all power except that inner power which was of God and which had encompassed all that is in heaven and on earth. How can I relate all that befell Him after He spoke these words? How shall I describe their heinous behaviour towards Him? They at last heaped on His blessed Person such woes that He took His flight unto the fourth Heaven.

It is also recorded in the Gospel according to St. Luke, that on a certain day Jesus passed by a Jew who was sick of the palsy, and lay upon a couch. When the Jew saw Him, he recognized Him, and cried out for His help. Jesus said unto him: "Arise from thy bed; thy sins are forgiven thee." Certain of the Jews, standing by, protested saying: "Who can forgive sins, but God alone?" And immediately He perceived their thoughts, Jesus answering said unto them: "Whether is it easier to say to the sick of the palsy, arise, and take up thy bed, and walk; or to say, thy sins are forgiven thee? that ye may know that the Son of Man hath power on earth to forgive sins." [1] This is the real sovereignty, and such is the power of God's chosen Ones! All these things which We have repeatedly mentioned, and the details which We have cited from divers sources, have no other purpose but to enable thee to grasp the meaning of the allusions in the utterances of the chosen Ones of God, lest certain of these utterances cause thy feet to falter and thy heart to be dismayed.

Thus with steadfast steps we may tread the Path of certitude, that perchance the breeze that bloweth from the meads of the good-pleasure of God may waft upon us the sweet savours of divine acceptance, and cause us, vanishing mortals that we are, to attain unto the Kingdom of everlasting glory. Then wilt thou comprehend the inner meaning of sovereignty and the like, spoken of in the tra-

[1] Cf. Luke 5:18–26.

ditions and scriptures. Furthermore, it is already evident and known unto thee that those things to which the Jews and the Christians have clung, and the cavilings which they heaped upon the Beauty of Muḥammad, the same have in this day been upheld by the people of the Qur'án, and been witnessed in their denunciations of the "Point of the Bayán"—may the souls of all that dwell within the kingdom of divine Revelations be a sacrifice unto Him! Behold their folly: they utter the selfsame words, uttered by the Jews of old, and know it not! How well and true are His words concerning them: "Leave them to entertain themselves with their cavilings!" [1] "As Thou livest, O Muḥammad! they are seized by the frenzy of their vain fancies." [2]

When the Unseen, the Eternal, the divine Essence, caused the Day-star of Muḥammad to rise above the horizon of knowledge, among the cavils which the Jewish divines raised against Him was that after Moses no Prophet should be sent of God. Yea, mention hath been made in the scriptures of a Soul Who must needs be made manifest and Who

[1] Qur'án 6:91.
[2] Qur'án 15:72.

will advance the Faith, and promote the interests of the people, of Moses, so that the Law of the Mosaic Dispensation may encompass the whole earth. Thus hath the King of eternal glory referred in His Book to the words uttered by those wanderers in the vale of remoteness and error: " 'The hand of God,' say the Jews, 'is chained up.' Chained up be their own hands! And for that which they have said, they were accursed. Nay, outstretched are both His hands!" [1] "The hand of God is above their hands." [2]

Although the commentators of the Qur'án have related in divers manners the circumstances attending the revelation of this verse, yet thou shouldst endeavour to apprehend the purpose thereof. He saith: How false is that which the Jews have imagined! How can the hand of him Who is the King in truth, Who caused the countenance of Moses to be made manifest, and conferred upon Him the robe of Prophethood—how can the hand of such a One be chained and fettered? How can He be conceived as powerless to raise up yet another Messenger after Moses? Behold the absurdity of

[1] Qur'án 5:64.
[2] Qur'án 48:10.

their saying; how far it hath strayed from the path
of knowledge and understanding! Observe how in
this day also, all these people have occupied themselves with such foolish absurdities. For over a
thousand years they have been reciting this verse,
and unwittingly pronouncing their censure against
the Jews, utterly unaware that they themselves,
openly and privily, are voicing the sentiments and
belief of the Jewish people! Thou art surely aware
of their idle contention, that all Revelation is
ended, that the portals of Divine mercy are closed,
that from the day-springs of eternal holiness no
sun shall rise again, that the Ocean of everlasting
bounty is forever stilled, and that out of the Tabernacle of ancient glory the Messengers of God have
ceased to be made manifest. Such is the measure
of the understanding of these small-minded, contemptible people. These people have imagined that
the flow of God's all-encompassing grace and plen-
teous mercies, the cessation of which no mind can
contemplate, has been halted. From every side
they have risen and girded up the loins of tyranny,
and exerted the utmost endeavour to quench with
the bitter waters of their vain fancy the flame
of God's burning Bush, oblivious that the globe
of power shall within its own mighty stronghold

protect the Lamp of God. The utter destitution into which this people have fallen doth surely suffice them, inasmuch as they have been deprived of the recognition of the essential Purpose and the knowledge of the Mystery and Substance of the Cause of God. For the highest and most excelling grace bestowed upon men is the grace of "attaining unto the Presence of God" and of His recognition, which has been promised unto all people. This is the utmost degree of grace vouchsafed unto man by the All-Bountiful, the Ancient of Days, and the fulness of His absolute bounty upon His creatures. Of this grace and bounty none of this people hath partaken, neither have they been honoured with this most exalted distinction. How numerous are those revealed verses which explicitly bear witness unto this most weighty truth and exalted Theme! And yet they have rejected it, and, after their own desire, misconstrued its meaning. Even as He hath revealed: "As for those who believe not in the signs of God, or that they shall ever meet Him, these of My mercy shall despair, and for them doth a grievous chastisement await." [1] Also He saith: "They who bear in mind that they shall attain unto the Presence of their Lord, and that unto Him

[1] Qur'án 29:23.

shall they return." [1] Also in another instance He
saith: "They who held it as certain that they must
meet God, said, 'How oft, by God's will, hath a
small host vanquished a numerous host!'" [2] In yet
another instance He revealeth: "Let him then who
hopeth to attain the presence of his Lord work a
righteous work." [3] And also He saith: "He order-
eth all things. He maketh His signs clear, that ye
may have firm faith in attaining the presence of
your Lord." [4]

This people have repudiated all these verses,
that unmistakably testify to the reality of "attainment unto the Divine Presence." No theme hath
been more emphatically asserted in the holy scriptures. Notwithstanding, they have deprived themselves of this lofty and most exalted rank, this supreme and glorious station. Some have contended
that by "attainment unto the Divine Presence" is
meant the "Revelation" of God in the Day of Resurrection. Should they assert that the "Revelation"
of God signifieth a "Universal Revelation," it is
clear and evident that such revelation already ex-
isteth in all things. The truth of this We have al-

---

[1] Qur'án 2:46.
[2] Qur'án 2:249.

[3] Qur'án 18:111.
[4] Qur'án 13:2.

ready established, inasmuch as We have demonstrated that all things are the recipients and revealers of the splendours of that ideal King, and that the signs of the revelation of that Sun, the Source of all splendour, exist and are manifest in the mirrors of beings. Nay, were man to gaze with the eye of divine and spiritual discernment, he will readily recognize that nothing whatsoever can exist without the revelation of the splendour of God, the ideal King. Consider how all created things eloquently testify to the revelation of that inner Light within them. Behold how within all things the portals of the Riḍván of God are opened, that seekers may attain the cities of understanding and wisdom, and enter the gardens of knowledge and power. Within every garden they will behold the mystic bride of inner meaning enshrined within the chambers of utterance in the utmost grace and fullest adornment. Most of the verses of the Qur'án indicate, and bear witness to, this spiritual theme. The verse: "Neither is there aught which doth not celebrate His praise" [1] is eloquent testimony thereto; and "We noted all things and wrote them down," [2] a faithful witness thereof. Now, if by

[1] Qur'án 17:44.
[2] Qur'án 78:29.

"attainment unto the Presence of God" is meant attainment unto the knowledge of such revelation, it is evident that all men have already attained unto the presence of the unchangeable Countenance of that peerless King. Why, then, restrict such revelation to the Day of Resurrection?

And were they to maintain that by "divine Presence" is meant the "Specific Revelation of God," expressed by certain Súfís as the "Most Holy Outpouring," if this be in the Essence Itself, it is evident that it hath been eternally in the divine Knowledge. Assuming the truth of this hypothesis, "attainment unto the divine Presence" is in this sense obviously possible to no one, inasmuch as this revelation is confined to the innermost Essence, unto which no man can attain. "The way is barred, and all seeking rejected." The minds of the favourites of heaven, however high they soar, can never attain this station, how much less the understanding of obscured and limited minds.

And were they to say that by "divine Presence" is meant the "Secondary Revelation of God," interpreted as the "Holy Outpouring," this is admittedly applicable to the world of creation, that is, in the realm of the primal and original manifestation of God. Such revelation is confined to His Prophets and chosen Ones, inasmuch as none mightier than they hath come to exist in the world of being. This truth all recognize, and bear witness thereto. These Prophets and chosen Ones of God are the recipients and revealers of all the unchangeable attributes and names of God. They are the mirrors that truly and faithfully reflect the light of God. Whatsoever is applicable to them is in reality applicable to God, Himself, Who is both the Visible and the Invisible. The knowledge of Him, Who is the Origin of all things, and attainment unto Him, are impossible save through knowledge of, and attainment unto, these luminous Beings who proceed from the Sun of Truth. By attaining, therefore, to the presence of these holy Luminaries, the "Presence of God" Himself is attained. From their knowledge, the knowledge of God is revealed, and from the light of their countenance, the splendour of the Face of God is made manifest. Through the manifold attributes of these Essences of Detachment, Who are both the first and the last, the seen and the hidden, it is made evident that He Who is the Sun of Truth is "the First and the Last, the Seen, and the

Hidden." [1] Likewise the other lofty names and exalted attributes of God. Therefore, whosoever, and in whatever Dispensation, hath recognized and attained unto the presence of these glorious, these resplendent and most excellent Luminaries, hath verily attained unto the "Presence of God" Himself, and entered the city of eternal and immortal life. Attainment unto such presence is possible only in the Day of Resurrection, which is the Day of the rise of God Himself through His all-embracing Revelation.

This is the meaning of the "Day of Resurrection," spoken of in all the scriptures, and announced unto all people. Reflect, can a more precious, a mightier, and more glorious day than this be conceived, so that man should willingly forego its grace, and deprive himself of its bounties, which like unto vernal showers are raining from the heaven of mercy upon all mankind? Having thus conclusively demonstrated that no day is greater than this Day, and no revelation more glorious than this Revelation, and having set forth all these weighty and infallible proofs which no understanding mind can question, and no man of learn-

[1] Qur'án 57:3.

ing overlook, how can man possibly, through the idle contention of the people of doubt and fancy, deprive himself of such a bountiful grace? Have they not heard the well-known tradition: "When the Qá'im riseth, that day is the Day of Resurrection?" In like manner, the Imáms, those unquenchable lights of divine guidance, have interpreted the verse: "What can such expect but that God should come down to them overshadowed with clouds," [1] —a sign which they have unquestionably regarded as one of the features of the Day of Resurrection —as referring to Qá'im and His manifestation.

Strive, therefore, O my brother, to grasp the meaning of "Resurrection," and cleanse thine ears from the idle sayings of these rejected people. Shouldst thou step into the realm of complete detachment, thou wilt readily testify that no day is mightier than this Day, and that no resurrection more awful than this Resurrection can ever be conceived. One righteous work performed in this Day, equalleth all the virtuous acts which for myriads of centuries men have practised—nay, We ask forgiveness of God for such a comparison! For verily the reward which such a deed deserveth is im-

[1] Qur'án 2:210.

mensely beyond and above the estimate of men. Inasmuch as these undiscerning and wretched souls have failed to apprehend the true meaning of "Resurrection" and of the "attainment unto the divine Presence," they therefore have remained utterly deprived of the grace thereof. Although the sole and fundamental purpose of all learning, and the toil and labour thereof, is attainment unto, and the recognition of, this station, yet they are all immersed in the pursuit of their material studies. They deny themselves every moment of leisure, and utterly ignore Him, Who is the Essence of all learning, and the one Object of their quest! Methinks, their lips have never touched the cup of divine Knowledge, nor do they seem to have attained even a dewdrop of the showers of heavenly grace.

Consider, how can he that faileth in the day of God's Revelation to attain unto the grace of the "Divine Presence" and to recognize His Manifestation, be justly called learned, though he may have spent æons in the pursuit of knowledge, and acquired all the limited and material learning of men? It is surely evident that he can in no wise be regarded as possessed of true knowledge. Whereas, the most unlettered of all men, if he be honoured with this supreme distinction, he verily is accounted as one of those divinely-learned men whose knowledge is of God; for such a man hath attained the acme of knowledge, and hath reached the furthermost summit of learning.

This station is also one of the signs of the Day of Revelation; even as it is said: "The abased amongst you, He shall exalt; and they that are exalted, He shall abase." And likewise, He hath revealed in the Qur'án: "And We desire to show favour to those who were brought low in the land, and to make them spiritual leaders among men, and to make of them Our heirs." [1] It hath been witnessed in this day how many of the divines, owing to their rejection of the Truth, have fallen into, and abide within, the uttermost depths of ignorance, and whose names have been effaced from the scroll of the glorious and learned. And how many of the ignorant who, by reason of their acceptance of the Faith, have soared aloft and attained the high summit of knowledge, and whose names have been inscribed by the Pen of Power upon the Tablet of divine Knowledge. Thus,

[1] Qur'án 28:5.

"What He pleaseth will God abrogate or confirm: for with Him is the Source of Revelation." [1] Therefore, it hath been said: "To seek evidence, when the Proof hath been established is but an unseemly act, and to be busied with the pursuit of knowledge when the Object of all learning hath been attained is truly blameworthy." Say O people of the earth! Behold this flamelike Youth that speedeth across the limitless profound of the Spirit, heralding unto you the tidings: "Lo: the Lamp of God is shining," and summoning you to heed His Cause which, though hidden beneath the veils of ancient splendour, shineth in the land of 'Iráq above the day-spring of eternal holiness.

O my friend, were the bird of thy mind to explore the heavens of the Revelation of the Qur'án, were it to contemplate the realm of divine knowledge unfolded therein, thou wouldst assuredly find unnumbered doors of knowledge set open before thee. Thou wouldst certainly recognize that all these things which have in this day hindered this people from attaining the shores of the ocean of eternal grace, the same things in the Muḥammadan

[1] Qur'án 13:41.

Dispensation prevented the people of that age from recognizing that divine Luminary, and from testifying to His truth. Thou wilt also apprehend the mysteries of "return" and "revelation," and wilt securely abide within the loftiest chambers of certitude and assurance.

And it came to pass that on a certain day a number of the opponents of that peerless Beauty, those that had strayed far from God's imperishable Sanctuary, scornfully spoke these words unto Muḥammad: "Verily, God hath entered into a covenant with us that we are not to credit an apostle until he present us a sacrifice which fire out of heaven shall devour." [1] The purport of this verse is that God hath covenanted with them that they should not believe in any messenger unless he work the miracle of Abel and Cain, that is, offer a sacrifice, and the fire from heaven consume it; even as they had heard it recounted in the story of Abel, which story is recorded in the scriptures. To this, Muḥammad, answering, said: "Already have Apostles before me come to you with sure testimonies, and with that of which ye speak. Wherefore slew ye them? Tell me, if ye are men

[1] Qur'án 3:183.

of truth."[1] And now, be fair; How could those people living in the days of Muḥammad have existed, thousands of years before, in the age of Adam or other Prophets? Why should Muḥammad, that Essence of truthfulness, have charged the people of His day with the murder of Abel or other Prophets? Thou hast none other alternative except to regard Muḥammad as an impostor or a fool—which God forbid!—or to maintain that those people of wickedness were the self-same people who in every age opposed and caviled at the Prophets and Messengers of God, till they finally caused them all to suffer martyrdom.

Ponder this in thine heart, that the sweet gales of divine knowledge, blowing from the meads of mercy, may waft upon thee the fragrance of the Beloved's utterance, and cause thy soul to attain the Riḍván of understanding. As the wayward of every age have failed to fathom the deeper import of these weighty and pregnant utterances, and imagined the answer of the Prophets of God to be irrelevant to the questions they asked them, they therefore have attributed ignorance and folly to those Essences of knowledge and understanding.

[1] Qur'án 3:182.

Likewise, Muḥammad, in another verse, uttereth His protest against the people of that age. He saith: "Although they had before prayed for victory over those who believed not, yet when there came unto them, He of Whom they had knowledge, they disbelieved in Him. The curse of God on the infidels!"[1] Reflect how this verse also implieth that the people living in the days of Muḥammad were the same people who in the days of the Prophets of old contended and fought in order to promote the Faith, and teach the Cause, of God. And yet, how could the generations living at the time of Jesus and Moses, and those who lived in the days of Muḥammad, be regarded as being actually one and the same people? Moreover, those whom they had formerly known were Moses, the Revealer of the Pentateuch, and Jesus, the Author of the Gospel. Notwithstanding, why did Muḥammad say: "When He of Whom they had knowledge came unto them"—that is Jesus or Moses—"they disbelieved in Him?" Was not Muḥammad to outward seeming called by a different name? Did He not come forth out of a different city? Did He not speak a different language, and reveal a different Law? How then can the truth of this

[1] Qur'án 2:89.

verse be established, and its meaning be made clear?

Strive therefore to comprehend the meaning of "return" which hath been so explicitly revealed in the Qur'án itself, and which none hath as yet understood. What sayest thou? If thou sayest that Muḥammad was the "return" of the Prophets of old, as is witnessed by this verse, His Companions must likewise be the "return" of the bygone Companions, even as the "return" of the former people is clearly attested by the text of the above-mentioned verses. And if thou deniest this, thou hast surely repudiated the truth of the Qur'án, the surest testimony of God unto men. In like manner, endeavour to grasp the significance of "return," "revelation," and "resurrection," as witnessed in the days of the Manifestations of the divine Essence, that thou mayest behold with thine own eyes the "return" of the holy souls into sanctified and illumined bodies, and mayest wash away the dust of ignorance, and cleanse the darkened self with the waters of mercy flowing from the Source of divine Knowledge; that perchance thou mayest, through the power of God and the light of divine guidance, distinguish the Morn of everlasting splendour from the darksome night of error.

Furthermore, it is evident to thee that the Bearers of the trust of God are made manifest unto the peoples of the earth as the Exponents of a new Cause and the Bearers of a new Message. Inasmuch as these Birds of the Celestial Throne are all sent down from the heaven of the Will of God, and as they all arise to proclaim His irresistible Faith, they therefore are regarded as one soul and the same person. For they all drink from the one Cup of the love of God, and all partake of the fruit of the same Tree of Oneness. These Manifestations of God have each a twofold station. One is the station of pure abstraction and essential unity. In this respect, if thou callest them all by one name, and dost ascribe to them the same attribute, thou hast not erred from the truth. Even as He hath revealed: "No distinction do We make between any of His Messengers!" [1] For they one and all summon the people of the earth to acknowledge the Unity of God, and herald unto them the Kawthar of an infinite grace and bounty. They are all invested with the robe of Prophethood, and honoured with the mantle of glory. Thus hath

[1] Qur'án 2:285.

Muḥammad, the Point of the Qur'án, revealed: "I am all the Prophets." Likewise, He saith: "I am the first Adam, Noah, Moses, and Jesus." Similar statements have been made by 'Alí. Sayings such as this, which indicate the essential unity of those Exponents of Oneness, have also emanated from the Channels of God's immortal utterance, and the Treasuries of the gems of divine knowledge, and have been recorded in the scriptures. These Countenances are the recipients of the Divine Command, and the day-springs of His Revelation. This Revelation is exalted above the veils of plurality and the exigencies of number. Thus He saith: "Our Cause is but one." [1] Inasmuch as the Cause is one and the same, the Exponents thereof also must needs be one and the same. Likewise, the Imáms of the Muḥammadan Faith, those lamps of certitude, have said: "Muḥammad is our first, Muḥammad our last, Muḥammad our all."

It is clear and evident to thee that all the Prophets are the Temples of the Cause of God, Who have appeared clothed in divers attire. If thou wilt observe with discriminating eyes, thou wilt behold them all abiding in the same tabernacle, soaring

[1] Qur'án 54:50.

in the same heaven, seated upon the same throne, uttering the same speech, and proclaiming the same Faith. Such is the unity of those Essences of being, those Luminaries of infinite and immeasurable splendour. Wherefore, should one of these Manifestations of Holiness proclaim saying: "I am the return of all the Prophets," He verily speaketh the truth. In like manner, in every subsequent Revelation, the return of the former Revelation is a fact, the truth of which is firmly established. Inasmuch as the return of the Prophets of God, as attested by verses and traditions, hath been conclusively demonstrated, the return of their chosen ones also is therefore definitely proven. This return is too manifest in itself to require any evidence or proof. For instance, consider that among the Prophets was Noah. When He was invested with the robe of Prophethood, and was moved by the Spirit of God to arise and proclaim His Cause, whoever believed in Him and acknowledged His Faith, was endowed with the grace of a new life. Of him it could be truly said that he was reborn and revived, inasmuch as previous to his belief in God and his acceptance of His Manifestation, he had set his affections on the things of the world, such as attachment to earthly goods, to wife, children, food, drink, and the like, so much so that in the day-time and in the night season his one concern had been to amass riches and procure for himself the means of enjoyment and pleasure. Aside from these things, before his partaking of the reviving waters of faith, he had been so wedded to the traditions of his forefathers, and so passionately devoted to the observance of their customs and laws, that he would have preferred to suffer death rather than violate one letter of those superstitious forms and manners current amongst his people. Even as the people have cried: "Verily we found our fathers with a faith, and verily, in their footsteps we follow." [1]

These same people, though wrapt in all these veils of limitation, and despite the restraint of such observances, as soon as they drank the immortal draught of faith, from the cup of certitude, at the hand of the Manifestation of the All-Glorious, were so transformed that they would renounce for His sake their kindred, their substance, their lives, their beliefs, yea, all else save God! So overpowering was their yearning for God, so uplifting their transports of ecstatic delight, that the world and

[1] Qur'án 43:22.

[155]

all that is therein faded before their eyes into nothingness. Have not this people exemplified the mysteries of "rebirth" and "return"? Hath it not been witnessed that these same people, ere they were endued with the new and wondrous grace of God, sought through innumerable devices, to ensure the protection of their lives against destruction? Would not a thorn fill them with terror, and the sight of a fox put them to flight? But once having been honoured with God's supreme distinction, and having been vouchsafed His bountiful grace, they would, if they were able, have freely offered up ten thousand lives in His path! Nay, their blessed souls, contemptuous of the cage of their bodies, would yearn for deliverance. A single warrior of that host would face and fight a multitude! And yet, how could they, but for the transformation wrought in their lives, be capable of manifesting such deeds which are contrary to the ways of men and incompatible with their worldly desires?

It is evident that nothing short of this mystic transformation could cause such spirit and behaviour, so utterly unlike their previous habits and manners, to be made manifest in the world of being. For their agitation was turned into peace, their doubt into certitude, their timidity into courage. Such is the potency of the Divine Elixir, which, swift as the twinkling of an eye, transmuteth the souls of men!

For instance, consider the substance of copper. Were it to be protected in its own mine from becoming solidified, it would, within the space of seventy years, attain to the state of gold. There are some, however, who maintain that copper itself is gold, which by becoming solidified is in a diseased condition, and hath not therefore reached its own state.

Be that as it may, the real elixir will, in one instant, cause the substance of copper to attain the state of gold, and will traverse the seventy-year stages in a single moment. Could this gold be called copper? Could it be claimed that it hath not attained the state of gold, whilst the touch-stone is at hand to assay it and distinguish it from copper?

Likewise, these souls, through the potency of the Divine Elixir, traverse, in the twinkling of an eye, the world of dust and advance into the realm of holiness; and with one step cover the earth of limitations and reach the domain of the Placeless. It behooveth thee to exert thine utmost to attain unto this Elixir which, in one fleeting breath, causeth the west of ignorance to reach the east of knowledge, illuminates the darkness of night with the resplendence of the morn, guideth the wanderer in the wilderness of doubt to the well-spring of the Divine Presence and Fount of certitude, and conferreth upon mortal souls the honour of acceptance into the Riḍván of immortality. Now, could this gold be thought to be copper, these people could likewise be thought to be the same as before they were endowed with faith.

O brother, behold how the inner mysteries of "rebirth," of "return," and of "resurrection" have each, through these all-sufficing, these unanswerable, and conclusive utterances, been unveiled and unravelled before thine eyes. God grant that through His gracious and invisible assistance, thou mayest divest thy body and soul of the old garment, and array thyself with the new and imperishable attire.

Therefore, those who in every subsequent Dispensation preceded the rest of mankind in embracing the Faith of God, who quaffed the clear waters of knowledge at the hand of the divine Beauty, and attained the loftiest summits of faith and certitude, these can be regarded, in name, in reality, in deeds, in words, and in rank, as the "return" of those who in a former Dispensation had achieved similar distinctions. For whatsoever the people of a former Dispensation have manifested, the same hath been shown by the people of this latter generation. Consider the rose: whether it blossometh in the East or in the West, it is none the less a rose. For what mattereth in this respect is not the outward shape and form of the rose, but rather the smell and fragrance which it doth impart.

Purge thy sight, therefore, from all earthly limitations, that thou mayest behold them all as the bearers of one Name, the exponents of one Cause, the manifestations of one Self, and the revealers of one Truth, and that thou mayest apprehend the mystic "return" of the Words of God as unfolded by these utterances. Reflect for a while upon the behaviour of the companions of the Muḥammadan Dispensation. Consider how, through the reviving breath of Muḥammad, they were cleansed from the defilements of earthly vanities, were delivered from selfish desires, and were detached from all else but Him. Behold how they preceded all the peoples of the earth in attaining unto His holy Presence—the Presence of God Himself—how they renounced the world and all that is therein, and sacrificed freely and joyously their lives at the feet of that Manifestation of the All-Glorious. And now, observe the "return" of the self-same determination, the self-same constancy and renunciation, manifested by the companions of the Point of the Bayán.[1] Thou hast witnessed how these companions have, through the wonders of the grace of the Lord of Lords, hoisted the standards of sublime renunciation upon the inaccessible heights of glory. These Lights have proceeded from but one Source, and these fruits are the fruits of one Tree. Thou canst discern neither difference nor distinction among them. All this is by the grace of God! On whom He will, He bestoweth His grace. Please God, that we avoid the land of denial, and advance into the ocean of acceptance, so that we may perceive, with an eye purged from all conflicting elements, the worlds of unity and diversity, of variation and oneness, of limitation and detachment, and wing our flight unto the highest and innermost sanctuary of the inner meaning of the Word of God.

[1] The Báb.

From these statements therefore it hath been made evident and manifest that should a Soul in the "End that knoweth no end" be made manifest, and arise to proclaim and uphold a Cause which in "the Beginning that hath no beginning" another Soul had proclaimed and upheld, it can be truly declared of Him Who is the Last and of Him Who was the First that they are one and the same, inasmuch as both are the Exponents of one and the same Cause. For this reason, hath the Point of the Bayán—may the life of all else but Him be His sacrifice!—likened the Manifestations of God unto the sun which, though it rise from the "Beginning that hath no beginning" until the "End that knoweth no end," is none the less the same sun. Now, wert thou to say, that this sun is the former sun, thou speakest the truth; and if thou sayest that this sun is the "return" of that sun, thou also speakest the truth. Likewise, from this statement it is made evident that the term "last" is applicable to the "first," and the term "first" applicable to the "last;" inasmuch as both the "first" and the "last" have risen to proclaim one and the same Faith.

Notwithstanding the obviousness of this theme, in the eyes of those that have quaffed the wine of knowledge and certitude, yet how many are those who, through failure to understand its meaning, have allowed the term "Seal of the Prophets" to obscure their understanding, and deprive them of the grace of all His manifold bounties! Hath not Muḥammad, Himself, declared: "I am all the Prophets?" Hath He not said as We have already mentioned: "I am Adam, Noah, Moses, and Jesus?" Why should Muḥammad, that immortal Beauty, Who hath said: "I am the first Adam" be incapable of saying also: "I am the last Adam"? For even as He regarded Himself to be the "First of the Prophets"—that is Adam—in like manner, the "Seal of the Prophets" is also applicable unto that Divine Beauty. It is admittedly obvious that being the "First of the Prophets," He likewise is their "Seal."

The mystery of this theme hath, in this Dispensation, been a sore test unto all mankind. Behold, how many are those who, clinging unto these words, have disbelieved Him Who is their true Revealer. What, We ask, could this people presume the terms "first" and "last"—when referring to God—glorified be His Name!—to mean? If they maintain that these terms bear reference to this material universe, how could it be possible, when the visible order of things is still manifestly existing? Nay, in this instance, by "first" is meant no other than the "last" and by "last" no other than the "first."

Even as in the "Beginning that hath no beginnings" the term "last" is truly applicable unto Him who is the Educator of the visible and of the invisible, in like manner, are the terms "first" and "last" applicable unto His Manifestations. They are at the same time the Exponents of both the "first" and the "last." Whilst established upon the seat of the "first," they occupy the throne of the "last." Were a discerning eye to be found, it will readily perceive that the exponents of the "first" and the "last," of the "manifest" and the "hidden," of the "beginning" and the "seal" are none other than these holy Beings, these Essences of Detachment, these divine Souls. And wert thou to soar in the holy realm of "God was alone, there was none else besides Him," thou wilt find in that Court all these names utterly non-existent and completely forgotten. Then will thine eyes no longer be obscured by these veils, these terms, and allusions. How ethereal and lofty is this station, unto which even Gabriel, unshepherded, can never attain, and the Bird of Heaven, unassisted, can never reach!

And, now, strive thou to comprehend the meaning of this saying of 'Alí, the Commander of the Faithful: "Piercing the veils of glory, unaided." Among these "veils of glory" are the divines and doctors living in the days of the Manifestation of God, who, because of their want of discernment and their love and eagerness for leadership, have failed to submit to the Cause of God, nay, have even refused to incline their ears unto the divine Melody. "They have thrust their fingers into their ears." [1] And the people also, utterly ignoring God and taking them for their masters, have placed themselves unreservedly under the authority of these pompous and hypocritical leaders, for they have no sight, no hearing, no heart, of their own to distinguish truth from falsehood.

Notwithstanding the divinely-inspired admonitions of all the Prophets, the Saints, and Chosen ones of God, enjoining the people to see with their own eyes and hear with their own ears, they have disdainfully rejected their counsels and have blindly followed, and will continue to follow, the

[1] Qur'án 2:19.

[164]

leaders of their Faith. Should a poor and obscure person, destitute of the attire of the men of learning, address them saying: "Follow ye, O people! the Messengers of God," [1] they would, greatly surprised at such a statement, reply: "What! Meanest thou that all these divines, all these exponents of learning, with all their authority, their pomp and pageantry, have erred, and failed to distinguish truth from falsehood? Dost thou, and people like thyself, pretend to have comprehended that which they have not understood?" If numbers and excellence of apparel be regarded as the criterions of learning and truth, the peoples of a bygone age, whom those of today have never surpassed in numbers, magnificence and power, should certainly be accounted a superior and worthier people.

It is clear and evident that whenever the Manifestations of Holiness were revealed, the divines of their day have hindered the people from attaining unto the way of truth. To this testify the records of all the scriptures and heavenly books. Not one Prophet of God was made manifest Who did not fall a victim to the relentless hate, to the denuncia-

[1] Qur'án 36:20.

tion, denial, and execration of the clerics of His day! Woe unto them for the iniquities their hands have formerly wrought! Woe unto them for that which they are now doing! What veils of glory more grievous than these embodiments of error! By the righteousness of God! to pierce such veils is the mightiest of all acts, and to rend them asunder the most meritorious of all deeds! May God assist us and assist you, O concourse of the Spirit! that perchance ye may in the time of His Manifestation be graciously aided to perform such deeds, and may in His days attain unto the Presence of God.

Furthermore, among the "veils of glory" are such terms as the "Seal of the Prophets" and the like, the removal of which is a supreme achievement in the sight of these base-born and erring souls. All, by reason of these mysterious sayings, these grievous "veils of glory," have been hindered from beholding the light of truth. Have they not heard the melody of that bird of Heaven,[1] uttering this mystery: "A thousand Fáṭimihs I have espoused, all of whom were the daughters of Muḥammad, Son of 'Abdu'lláh, the 'Seal of the

[1] Imám 'Alí.

[166]

Prophets?'" Behold, how many are the mysteries that lie as yet unravelled within the tabernacle of the knowledge of God, and how numerous the gems of His wisdom that are still concealed in His inviolable treasuries! Shouldest thou ponder this in thine heart, thou wouldst realize that His handiwork knoweth neither beginning nor end. The domain of His decree is too vast for the tongue of mortals to describe, or for the bird of the human mind to traverse; and the dispensations of His providence are too mysterious for the mind of man to comprehend. His creation no end hath overtaken, and it hath ever existed from the "Beginning that hath no beginning"; and the Manifestations of His Beauty no beginning hath beheld, and they will continue to the "End that knoweth no end." Ponder this utterance in thine heart, and reflect how it is applicable unto all these holy Souls.

Likewise, strive thou to comprehend the meaning of the melody of that eternal beauty, Ḥusayn, son of 'Alí, who, addressing Salmán, spoke words such as these: "I was with a thousand Adams, the interval between each and the next Adam was fifty thousand years, and to each one of these I declared the Successorship conferred upon my father." He then recounteth certain details, until he saith: "I have fought one thousand battles in the path of God, the least and most insignificant of which was like the battle of Khaybar, in which battle my father fought and contended against the infidels." Endeavour now to apprehend from these two traditions the mysteries of "end," "return," and "creation without beginning or end."

O my beloved! Immeasurably exalted is the celestial Melody above the strivings of human ear to hear or mind to grasp its mystery! How can the helpless ant step into the court of the All-Glorious? And yet, feeble souls, through lack of understanding, reject these abstruse utterances, and question the truth of such traditions. Nay, none can comprehend them save those that are possessed of an understanding heart. Say, He is that End for Whom no end in all the universe can be imagined, and for Whom no beginning in the world of creation can be conceived. Behold, O concourse of the earth, the splendours of the End, revealed in the Manifestations of the Beginning!

How strange! These people with one hand cling to those verses of the Qur'án and those traditions

of the people of certitude which they have found
to accord with their inclinations and interests, and
with the other reject those which are contrary to
their selfish desires. "Believe ye then part of the
Book, and deny part?" [1] How could ye judge that
which ye understand not? Even as the Lord of
being hath in His unerring Book, after speaking of
the "Seal" in His exalted utterance: "Muḥammad
is the Apostle of God and the Seal of the Prophets," [2] hath revealed unto all people the promise
of "attainment unto the divine Presence." To this
attainment to the presence of the immortal King
testify the verses of the Book, some of which We
have already mentioned. The one true God is My
witness! Nothing more exalted or more explicit
than "attainment unto the divine Presence" hath
been revealed in the Qur'án. Well is it with him
that hath attained thereunto, in the day wherein
most of the people, even as ye witness, have turned
away therefrom.

And yet, through the mystery of the former
verse, they have turned away from the grace promised by the latter, despite the fact that "attainment
unto the divine Presence" in the "Day of Resur-

[1] Qur'án 2:85.
[2] Qur'án 33:40.

rection" is explicitly stated in the Book. It hath been demonstrated and definitely established, through clear evidences, that by "Resurrection" is meant the rise of the Manifestation of God to proclaim His Cause, and by "attainment unto the divine Presence" is meant attainment unto the presence of His Beauty in the person of His Manifestation. For verily, "No vision taketh in Him, but He taketh in all vision." [1] Notwithstanding all these indubitable facts and lucid statements, they have foolishly clung to the term "seal," and remained utterly deprived of the recognition of Him Who is the Revealer of both the Seal and the Beginning, in the day of His presence. "If God should chastise men for their perverse doings, He would not leave upon the earth a moving thing! But to an appointed time doth He respite them." [2] But apart from all these things, had this people attained unto a drop of the crystal streams flowing from the words: "God doeth whatsoever He willeth, and ordaineth whatsoever He pleaseth," they would not have raised any unseemly cavils, such as these, against the focal Center of His Revelation. The Cause of God, all deeds and words, are held

[1] Qur'án 6:103.
[2] Qur'án 16:61.

within the grasp of His power. "All things lie imprisoned within the hollow of His mighty Hand; all things are easy and possible unto Him." He accomplisheth whatsoever He willeth, and doeth all that He desireth. "Whoso sayeth 'why' or 'wherefore' hath spoken blasphemy!" Were these people to shake off the slumber of negligence and realize that which their hands have wrought, they would surely perish, and would of their own accord cast themselves into fire—their end and real abode. Have they not heard that which He hath revealed: "He shall not be asked of His doings?" [1] In the light of these utterances, how can man be so bold as to question Him, and busy himself with idle sayings?

Gracious God! So great is the folly and perversity of the people, that they have turned their face toward their own thoughts and desires, and have turned their back upon the knowledge and will of God—hallowed and glorified be His name!

Be fair: Were these people to acknowledge the truth of these luminous words and holy allusions, and recognize God as "Him that doeth whatsoever He pleaseth," how could they continue to cleave

[1] Qur'án 21:23.

unto these glaring absurdities? Nay, with all their soul, they would accept and submit to whatsoever He saith. I swear by God! But for the divine Decree, and the inscrutable dispensations of Providence, the earth itself would have utterly destroyed all this people! "He will, however, respite them until the appointed time of a known day."

Twelve hundred and eighty years have passed since the dawn of the Muḥammadan Dispensation, and with every break of day, these blind and ignoble people have recited their Qur'án, and yet have failed to grasp one letter of that Book! Again and again they read those verses which clearly testify to the reality of these holy themes, and bear witness to the truth of the Manifestations of eternal Glory, and still apprehend not their purpose. They have even failed to realize, all this time, that, in every age, the reading of the scriptures and holy books is for no other purpose except to enable the reader to apprehend their meaning and unravel their innermost mysteries. Otherwise reading, without understanding, is of no abiding profit unto man.

And it came to pass that on a certain day a needy man came to visit this Soul, craving for the ocean of His knowledge. While conversing with him, mention was made concerning the signs of the Day of Judgment, Resurrection, Revival, and Reckoning. He urged Us to explain how, in this wondrous Dispensation, the peoples of the world were brought to a reckoning, when none were made aware of it. Thereupon, We imparted unto him, according to the measure of his capacity and understanding, certain truths of Science and ancient Wisdom. We then asked him saying: "Hast thou not read the Qur'án, and art thou not aware of this blessed verse: 'On that day shall neither man nor spirit be asked of his Sin?'[1] Dost thou not realize that by 'asking' is not meant asking by tongue or speech, even as the verse itself doth indicate and prove? For afterward it is said: 'By their countenance shall the sinners be known, and they shall be seized by their forelocks and their feet.' "[2]

Thus the peoples of the world are judged by their countenance. By it, their misbelief, their faith, and their iniquity are all made manifest. Even as it is evident in this day how the people of error are, by their countenance, known and dis-

[1] Qur'án 55:39.
[2] Qur'án 55:41.

tinguished from the followers of divine Guidance. Were these people, wholly for the sake of God and with no desire but His good-pleasure, to ponder the verses of the Book in their heart, they would of a certainty find whatsoever they seek. In its verses would they find revealed and manifest all the things, be they great or small, that have come to pass in this Dispensation. They would even recognize in them references unto the departure of the Manifestations of the names and attributes of God from out their native land; to the opposition and disdainful arrogance of government and people; and to the dwelling and establishment of the Universal Manifestation in an appointed and specially designated land. No man, however, can comprehend this except he who is possessed of an understanding heart.

We seal Our theme with that which was formerly revealed unto Muḥammad that the seal thereof may shed the fragrance of that holy musk which leadeth men unto the Riḍván of unfading splendour. He said, and His Word is the truth: "And God calleth to the Abode of Peace;[1] and He guideth whom He will into the right way."[2]

[1] Baghdád.
[2] Qur'án 10:25.

"For them is an Abode of Peace with their Lord! and He shall be their Protector because of their works." [1] This He hath revealed that His grace may encompass the world. Praise be to God, the Lord of all being!

We have variously and repeatedly set forth the meaning of every theme, that perchance every soul, whether high or low, may obtain, according to his measure and capacity, his share and portion thereof. Should he be unable to comprehend a certain argument, he may, thus, by referring unto another, attain his purpose. "That all sorts of men may know where to quench their thirst."

By God! This Bird of Heaven, now dwelling upon the dust, can, besides these melodies, utter a myriad songs, and is able, apart from these utterances, to unfold innumerable mysteries. Every single note of its unpronounced utterances is immeasurably exalted above all that hath already been revealed, and immensely glorified beyond that which hath streamed from this Pen. Let the future disclose the hour when the Brides of inner meaning, will, as decreed by the Will of God, hasten forth, unveiled, out of their mystic man-

[1] Qur'án 6:127.

sions, and manifest themselves in the ancient realm of being. Nothing whatsoever is possible without His permission; no power can endure save through His power, and there is none other God but He. His is the world of creation, and His the Cause of God. All proclaim His Revelation, and all unfold the mysteries of His Spirit.

We have already in the foregoing pages assigned two stations unto each of the Luminaries arising from the Daysprings of eternal holiness. One of these stations, the station of essential unity, We have already explained. "No distinction do We make between any of them." [1] The other is the station of distinction, and pertaineth to the world of creation and to the limitations thereof. In this respect, each Manifestation of God hath a distinct individuality, a definitely prescribed mission, a predestined Revelation, and specially designated limitations. Each one of them is known by a different name, is characterized by a special attribute, fulfils a definite Mission, and is entrusted with a particular Revelation. Even as He saith: "Some of the Apostles We have caused to excel the others. To some God hath spoken, some He hath raised and exalted. And to Jesus, Son of Mary, We gave

[1] Qur'án 2:136.

[176]

manifest signs, and We strengthened Him with the Holy Spirit." [1]

It is because of this difference in their station and mission that the words and utterances flowing from these Well-springs of divine knowledge appear to diverge and differ. Otherwise, in the eyes of them that are initiated into the mysteries of divine wisdom, all their utterances are in reality but the expressions of one Truth. As most of the people have failed to appreciate those stations to which We have referred, they therefore feel perplexed and dismayed at the varying utterances pronounced by Manifestations that are essentially one and the same.

It hath ever been evident that all these divergences of utterance are attributable to differences of station. Thus, viewed from the standpoint of their oneness and sublime detachment, the attributes of Godhead, Divinity, Supreme Singleness, and Inmost Essence, have been and are applicable to those Essences of being, inasmuch as they all abide on the throne of divine Revelation, and are established upon the seat of divine Concealment. Through their appearance the Revelation of God

[1] Qur'án 2:253.

is made manifest, and by their countenance the Beauty of God is revealed. Thus it is that the accents of God Himself have been heard uttered by these Manifestations of the divine Being.

Viewed in the light of their second station—the station of distinction, differentiation, temporal limitations, characteristics and standards,—they manifest absolute servitude, utter destitution and complete self-effacement. Even as He saith: "I am the servant of God.[1] I am but a man like you."[2]

From these incontrovertible and fully demonstrated statements strive thou to apprehend the meaning of the questions thou hast asked, that thou mayest become steadfast in the Faith of God, and not be dismayed by the divergences in the utterances of His Prophets and Chosen Ones.

Were any of the all-embracing Manifestations of God to declare: "I am God!" He verily speaketh the truth, and no doubt attacheth thereto. For it hath been repeatedly demonstrated that through their Revelation, their attributes and names, the Revelation of God, His name and His attributes, are made manifest in the world. Thus, He hath revealed: "Those shafts were God's, not

[1] Qur'án 19:31.   [2] Qur'án 18:110.

[178]

Thine!"[1] And also He saith: "In truth, they who
plighted fealty unto thee, really plighted that
fealty unto God."[2] And were any of them to voice
the utterance: "I am the Messenger of God," He
also speaketh the truth, the indubitable truth. Even
as He saith: "Muḥammad is not the father of any
man among you, but He is the Messenger of
God."[3] Viewed in this light, they are all but Messengers of that ideal King, that unchangeable Essence. And were they all to proclaim: "I am the
Seal of the Prophets," they verily utter but the
truth, beyond the faintest shadow of doubt. For
they are all but one person, one soul, one spirit,
one being, one revelation. They are all the manifestation of the "Beginning" and the "End," the
"First" and the "Last," the "Seen" and "Hidden"
—all of which pertain to Him Who is the innermost Spirit of Spirits and eternal Essence of Essences. And were they to say: "We are the servants
of God," this also is a manifest and indisputable
fact. For they have been made manifest in the
uttermost state of servitude, a servitude the like of
which no man can possibly attain. Thus in mo-
ments in which these Essences of being were deeply

[1] Qur'án 8:17.　　　　　　[3] Qur'án 33:40.
[2] Qur'án 48:10.

immersed beneath the oceans of ancient and everlasting holiness, or when they soared to the loftiest summits of divine mysteries, they claimed their utterance to be the Voice of divinity, the Call of God Himself. Were the eye of discernment to be opened, it would recognize that in this very state, they have considered themselves utterly effaced and non-existent in the face of Him Who is the All-Pervading, the Incorruptible. Methinks, they have regarded themselves as utter nothingness, and deemed their mention in that Court an act of blasphemy. For the slightest whispering of self, within such a Court, is an evidence of self-assertion and independent existence. In the eyes of them that have attained unto that Court, such a suggestion is itself a grievous transgression. How much more grievous would it be, were aught else to be mentioned in that Presence, were man's heart, his tongue, his mind, or his soul, to be busied with anyone but the Well-Beloved, were his eyes to behold any countenance other than His beauty, were his ear to be inclined to any melody but His voice, and were his feet to tread any way but His way.

In this day the breeze of God is wafted, and His Spirit hath pervaded all things. Such is the outpouring of His grace that the pen is stilled and the tongue is speechless.

By virtue of this station, they have claimed for themselves the Voice of Divinity and the like, whilst by virtue of their station of Messengership, they have declared themselves the Messengers of God. In every instance they have voiced an utterance that would conform to the requirements of the occasion, and have ascribed all these declarations to Themselves, declarations ranging from the realm of divine Revelation to the realm of creation, and from the domain of Divinity even unto the domain of earthly existence. Thus it is that whatsoever be their utterance, whether it pertain to the realm of Divinity, Lordship, Prophethood, Messengership, Guardianship, Apostleship or Servitude, all is true, beyond the shadow of a doubt. Therefore, these sayings which We have quoted in support of Our argument must be attentively considered, that the divergent utterances of the Manifestations of the Unseen and Daysprings of Holiness may cease to agitate the soul and perplex the mind.

Those words uttered by the Luminaries of Truth must needs be pondered, and should their significance be not grasped, enlightenment should be sought from the Trustees of the depositories of Knowledge, that these may expound their meaning, and unravel their mystery. For it behooveth no man to interpret the holy words according to his own imperfect understanding, nor, having found them to be contrary to his inclination and desires, to reject and repudiate their truth. For such, to-day, is the manner of the divines and doctors of the age, who occupy the seats of knowledge and learning, and who have named ignorance knowledge, and called oppression justice. Were these to ask the Light of Truth concerning those images which their idle fancy hath carved, and were they to find His answer inconsistent with their own conceptions and their own understanding of the Book, they would assuredly denounce Him Who is the Mine and Wellhead of all Knowledge as the very negation of understanding. Such things have happened in every age.

For instance, when Muḥammad, the Lord of being, was questioned concerning the new moons, He, as bidden by God, made reply: "They are periods appointed unto men." [1] Thereupon, they

[1] Qur'án 2:189.

that heard Him denounced Him as an ignorant man.

Likewise, in the verse concerning the "Spirit," He saith: "And they will ask Thee of the Spirit. Say, 'the Spirit proceedeth at My Lord's command.'" [1] As soon as Muḥammad's answer was given, they all clamorously protested, saying: "Lo! an ignorant man who knoweth not what the Spirit is, calleth Himself the Revealer of divine Knowledge!" And now behold the divines of the age who, because of their being honoured by His name, and finding that their fathers have acknowledged His Revelation, have blindly submitted to His truth. Observe, were this people today to receive such answers in reply to such questionings, they would unhesitatingly reject and denounce them—nay, they would again utter the self-same cavils, even as they have uttered them in this day. All this, notwithstanding the fact that these Essences of being are immensely exalted above such fanciful images, and are immeasurably glorified beyond all these vain sayings and above the comprehension of every understanding heart. Their so-called learning, when compared with that Knowledge, is utter falsehood, and all their understanding naught but

[1] Qur'án 17:85.

blatant error. Nay, whatsoever proceedeth from these Mines of divine Wisdom and these Treasuries of eternal knowledge is truth, and naught else but the truth. The saying: "Knowledge is one point, which the foolish have multiplied" is a proof of Our argument, and the tradition: "Knowledge is a light which God sheddeth into the heart of whomsoever He willeth" a confirmation of Our statement.

Inasmuch as they have not apprehended the meaning of Knowledge, and have called by that name those images fashioned by their own fancy and which have sprung from the embodiments of ignorance, they therefore have inflicted upon the Source of Knowledge that which thou hast heard and witnessed.

For instance, a certain man,[1] reputed for his learning and attainments, and accounting himself as one of the pre-eminent leaders of his people, hath in his book denounced and vilified all the exponents of true learning. This is made abundantly clear by his explicit statements as well as by his allusions throughout his book. As We had frequently heard about him, We purposed to read

[1] Ḥájí Mírzá Karím Khán.

[184]

some of his works. Although We never felt disposed to peruse other peoples' writings, yet as some had questioned Us concerning him, We felt it necessary to refer to his books, in order that We might answer Our questioners with knowledge and understanding. His works, in the Arabic tongue, were, however, not available, until one day a certain man informed Us that one of his compositions, entitled Irshádu'l-'Avám,[1] could be found in this city. From this title We perceived the odour of conceit and vainglory, inasmuch as he hath imagined himself a learned man and regarded the rest of the people ignorant. His worth was in fact made known by the very title he had chosen for his book. It became evident that its author was following the path of self and desire, and was lost in the wilderness of ignorance and folly. Methinks, he had forgotten the well-known tradition which sayeth: "Knowledge is all that is knowable; and might and power, all creation." Notwithstanding, We sent for the book, and kept it with Us a few days. It was probably referred to twice. The second time, We accidentally came upon the story of the "Mi'ráj"[2] of Muḥammad, of

[1] "Guidance unto the ignorant."
[2] Ascent.

Whom was spoken: "But for Thee, I would not have created the spheres." We noticed that he had enumerated some twenty or more sciences, the knowledge of which he considered to be essential for the comprehension of the mystery of the "Mi'ráj". We gathered from his statements that unless a man be deeply versed in them all, he can never attain to a proper understanding of this transcendent and exalted theme. Among the specified sciences were the science of metaphysical abstractions, of alchemy, and natural magic. Such vain and discarded learnings, this man hath regarded as the pre-requisites of the understanding of the sacred and abiding mysteries of divine Knowledge.

Gracious God! Such is the measure of his understanding. And yet, behold what cavils and calumnies he hath heaped upon those Embodiments of God's infinite knowledge! How well and true is the saying: "Flingest thou thy calumnies unto the face of Them Whom the one true God hath made the Trustees of the treasures of His seventh sphere?" Not one understanding heart or mind, not one among the wise and learned, hath taken notice of these preposterous statements. And yet, how clear and evident it is to every discerning heart that this so-called learning is and hath ever been, rejected by Him Who is the one true God. How can the knowledge of these sciences, which are so contemptible in the eyes of the truly learned, be regarded as essential to the apprehension of the mysteries of the "Mi'ráj," whilst the Lord of the "Mi'ráj" Himself was never burdened with a single letter of these limited and obscure learnings, and never defiled His radiant heart with any of these fanciful illusions? How truly hath he said: "All human attainment moveth upon a lame ass, whilst Truth, riding upon the wind, darteth across space." By the righteousness of God! Whoso desireth to fathom the mystery of this "Mi'ráj," and craveth a drop from this ocean, if the mirror of his heart be already obscured by the dust of these learnings, he must needs cleanse and purify it ere the light of this mystery can be reflected therein.

In this day, they that are submerged beneath the ocean of ancient Knowledge, and dwell within the ark of divine wisdom, forbid the people such idle pursuits. Their shining breasts are, praise be to God, sanctified from every trace of such learning, and are exalted above such grievous veils. We have

[187]

consumed this densest of all veils, with the fire of the love of the Beloved—the veil referred to in the saying: "The most grievous of all veils is the veil of knowledge." Upon its ashes, We have reared the tabernacle of divine knowledge. We have, praise be to God, burned the "veils of glory" with the fire of the beauty of the Best-Beloved. We have driven from the human heart all else but Him Who is the Desire of the world, and glory therein. We cleave to no knowledge but His Knowledge, and set our hearts on naught save the effulgent glories of His light.

We were surprised exceedingly when We observed that his one purpose was to make the people realize that all these learnings were possessed by him. And yet, I swear by God that not one breath, blowing from the meads of divine knowledge, hath ever been wafted upon his soul, nor hath he ever unravelled a single mystery of ancient wisdom. Nay, were the meaning of Knowledge ever to be expounded unto him, dismay would fill his heart, and his whole being would shake to its foundation. Notwithstanding his base and senseless statements, behold to what heights of extravagance his claims have reached!

Gracious God! How great is Our amazement at the way the people have gathered around him, and have borne allegiance to his person! Content with transient dust, these people have turned their face unto it, and cast behind their backs Him Who is the Lord of Lords. Satisfied with the croaking of the crow and enamoured with the visage of the raven, they have renounced the melody of the nightingale and the charm of the rose. What unspeakable fallacies the perusal of this pretentious book hath revealed! They are too unworthy for any pen to describe, and too base for one moment's attention. Should a touchstone be found, however, it would instantly distinguish truth from falsehood, light from darkness, and sun from shadow.

Among the sciences which this pretender hath professed is that of alchemy. We cherish the hope that either a king or a man of preeminent power may call upon him to translate this science from the realm of fancy to the domain of fact and from the plane of mere pretension to that of actual achievement. Would that this unlearned and humble Servant, who never laid any pretension to such things, nor even regarded them as the criterion of true knowledge, might undertake the same task, that thereby the truth might be known and distinguished from falsehood. But of what avail! All this generation could offer Us were wounds from its darts, and the only cup it proffered to Our lips was the cup of its venom. On our neck We still bear the scar of chains, and upon Our body are imprinted the evidences of an unyielding cruelty.

And as to this man's attainments, his ignorance, understanding and belief, behold what the Book which embraceth all things hath revealed; "Verily, the tree of Zaqqúm [1] shall be the food of the Athím." [2] And then follow certain verses, until He saith: "Taste this, for thou forsooth art the mighty Karím!" [3] Consider how clearly and explicitly he hath been described in God's incorruptible Book! This man, moreover, feigning humility, hath in his own book referred to himself as the "athím servant": "Athím" in the Book of God, mighty among the common herd, "Karím" in name!

Ponder the blessed verse, so that the meaning of the words: "There is neither a thing green nor sere

[1] Infernal tree.
[2] Sinner or sinful. Qur'án 44:43-44.
[3] Honourable—Qur'án 44:49.

but it is noted in the unerring Book," [1] may be imprinted upon the tablet of thy heart. Notwithstanding, a multitude bear him allegiance. They have rejected the Moses of knowledge and justice, and clung to the Sámirí [2] of ignorance. They have turned away their eyes from the Day-star of truth which shineth in the divine and everlasting heaven, and have utterly ignored its splendour.

O my brother! A divine Mine only can yield the gems of divine knowledge, and the fragrance of the mystic Flower can be inhaled only in the ideal Garden, and the lilies of ancient wisdom can blossom nowhere except in the city of a stainless heart. "In a rich soil, its plants spring forth abundantly by permission of its Lord, and in that soil which is bad, they spring forth but scantily." [3]

Inasmuch as it hath been clearly shown that only those who are initiated into the divine mysteries can comprehend the melodies uttered by the Bird of Heaven, it is therefore incumbent upon every one to seek enlightenment from the illumined in heart and from the Treasuries of divine mysteries

[1] Qur'án 6:59.
[2] A magician contemporary with Moses.
[3] Qur'án 7:57.

regarding the intricacies of God's Faith and the abstruse allusions in the utterances of the Day-springs of Holiness. Thus will these mysteries be unravelled, not by the aid of acquired learning, but solely through the assistance of God and the outpourings of His grace. "Ask ye, therefore, of them that have the custody of the Scriptures, if ye know it not." [1]

But, O my brother, when a true seeker determineth to take the step of search in the path leading to the knowledge of the Ancient of Days, he must, before all else, cleanse and purify his heart, which is the seat of the revelation of the inner mysteries of God, from the obscuring dust of all acquired knowledge, and the allusions of the embodiments of satanic fancy. He must purge his breast, which is the sanctuary of the abiding love of the Beloved, of every defilement, and sanctify his soul from all that pertaineth to water and clay, from all shadowy and ephemeral attachments. He must so cleanse his heart that no remnant of either love or hate may linger therein, lest that love blindly incline him to error, or that hate repel him away from the truth. Even as thou dost witness in this

[1] Qur'án 16:43.

day how most of the people, because of such love and hate, are bereft of the immortal Face, have strayed far from the Embodiments of the divine mysteries, and, shepherdless, are roaming through the wilderness of oblivion and error. That seeker must at all times put his trust in God, must renounce the peoples of the earth, detach himself from the world of dust, and cleave unto Him Who is the Lord of Lords. He must never seek to exalt himself above any one, must wash away from the tablet of his heart every trace of pride and vainglory, must cling unto patience and resignation, observe silence, and refrain from idle talk. For the tongue is a smouldering fire, and excess of speech a deadly poison. Material fire consumeth the body, whereas the fire of the tongue devoureth both heart and soul. The force of the former lasteth but for a time, whilst the effects of the latter endure a century.

That seeker should also regard backbiting as grievous error, and keep himself aloof from its dominion, inasmuch as backbiting quencheth the light of the heart, and extinguisheth the life of the soul. He should be content with little, and be freed from all inordinate desire. He should treasure the companionship of those that have renounced the world, and regard avoidance of boastful and worldly people a precious benefit. At the dawn of every day he should commune with God, and with all his soul persevere in the quest of his Beloved. He should consume every wayward thought with the flame of His loving mention, and, with the swiftness of lightning, pass by all else save Him. He should succour the dispossessed, and never withhold his favour from the destitute. He should show kindness to animals, how much more unto his fellow-man, to him who is endowed with the power of utterance. He should not hesitate to offer up his life for his Beloved, nor allow the censure of the people to turn him away from the Truth. He should not wish for others that which he doth not wish for himself, nor promise that which he doth not fulfil. With all his heart should the seeker avoid fellowship with evil doers, and pray for the remission of their sins. He should forgive the sinful, and never despise his low estate, for none knoweth what his own end shall be. How often hath a sinner, at the hour of death, attained to the essence of faith, and, quaffing the immortal draught, hath taken his flight unto the celestial Concourse. And how often hath a devout believer, at the hour of his soul's ascension, been so changed as to fall into the nethermost fire. Our purpose in revealing these convincing and weighty utterances is to impress upon the seeker that he should regard all else beside God as transient, and count all things save Him, Who is the Object of all adoration, as utter nothingness.

These are among the attributes of the exalted, and constitute the hall-mark of the spiritually-minded. They have already been mentioned in connection with the requirements of the wayfarers that tread the Path of Positive Knowledge. When the detached wayfarer and sincere seeker hath fulfilled these essential conditions, then and only then can he be called a true seeker. Whensoever he hath fulfilled the conditions implied in the verse: "Whoso maketh efforts for Us," [1] he shall enjoy the blessing conferred by the words: "In Our ways shall We assuredly guide him." [2]

Only when the lamp of search, of earnest striving, of longing desire, of passionate devotion, of fervid love, of rapture, and ecstasy, is kindled within the seeker's heart, and the breeze of His

[1] Qur'án 29:69.
[2] Ibid.

loving-kindness is wafted upon his soul, will the darkness of error be dispelled, the mists of doubts and misgivings be dissipated, and the lights of knowledge and certitude envelop his being. At that hour will the mystic Herald, bearing the joyful tidings of the Spirit, shine forth from the City of God resplendent as the morn, and, through the trumpet-blast of knowledge, will awaken the heart, the soul, and the spirit from the slumber of negligence. Then will the manifold favours and outpouring grace of the holy and everlasting Spirit confer such new life upon the seeker that he will find himself endowed with a new eye, a new ear, a new heart, and a new mind. He will contemplate the manifest signs of the universe, and will penetrate the hidden mysteries of the soul. Gazing with the eye of God, he will perceive within every atom a door that leadeth him to the stations of absolute certitude. He will discover in all things the mysteries of divine Revelation and the evidences of an everlasting manifestation.

I swear by God! Were he that treadeth the path of guidance and seeketh to scale the heights of righteousness to attain unto this glorious and supreme station, he would inhale at a distance of a thousand leagues the fragrance of God, and would perceive the resplendent morn of a divine Guidance rising above the dayspring of all things. Each and every thing, however small, would be to him a revelation, leading him to his Beloved, the Object of his quest. So great shall be the discernment of this seeker that he will discriminate between truth and falsehood even as he doth distinguish the sun from shadow. If in the uttermost corners of the East the sweet savours of God be wafted, he will assuredly recognize and inhale their fragrance, even though he be dwelling in the uttermost ends of the West. He will likewise clearly distinguish all the signs of God—His wondrous utterances, His great works, and mighty deeds—from the doings, words and ways of men, even as the jeweller who knoweth the gem from the stone, or the man who distinguisheth the spring from autumn and heat from cold. When the channel of the human soul is cleansed of all worldly and impeding attachments, it will unfailingly perceive the breath of the Beloved across immeasurable distances, and will, led by its perfume, attain and enter the City of Certitude. Therein he will discern the wonders of His ancient wisdom, and will perceive all the hidden teachings from the rustling leaves of the Tree—which flourisheth in that City. With both his inner and his outer ear he will hear from its dust the hymns of glory and praise ascending unto the Lord of Lords, and with his inner eye will he discover the mysteries of "return" and "revival." How unspeakably glorious are the signs, the tokens, the revelations, and splendours which He Who is the King of names and attributes hath destined for that City! The attainment of this City quencheth thirst without water, and kindleth the love of God without fire. Within every blade of grass are enshrined the mysteries of an inscrutable wisdom, and upon every rosebush a myriad nightingales pour out, in blissful rapture, their melody. Its wondrous tulips unfold the mystery of the undying Fire in the Burning Bush, and its sweet savours of holiness breathe the perfume of the Messianic Spirit. It bestoweth wealth without gold, and conferreth immortality without death. In every leaf ineffable delights are treasured, and within every chamber unnumbered mysteries lie hidden.

They that valiantly labour in quest of God's will, when once they have renounced all else but Him, will be so attached and wedded to that City that a moment's separation from it would to them be unthinkable. They will hearken unto infallible proofs from the Hyacinth of that assembly, and receive the surest testimonies from the beauty of its Rose and the melody of its Nightingale. Once in about a thousand years shall this City be renewed and re-adorned.

Wherefore, O my friend, it behooveth Us to exert the highest endeavour to attain unto that City, and, by the grace of God and His loving-kindness, rend asunder the "veils of glory"; so that, with inflexible steadfastness, we may sacrifice our drooping souls in the path of the New Beloved. We should with tearful eyes, fervently and repeatedly, implore Him to grant us the favour of that grace. That city is none other than the Word of God revealed in every age and dispensation. In the days of Moses it was the Pentateuch; in the days of Jesus the Gospel; in the days of Muḥammad the Messenger of God the Qur'án; in this day the Bayán; and in the dispensation of Him Whom God will make manifest His own Book—the Book unto which all the Books of former Dispensations must needs be referred, the Book which standeth amongst them all transcen-

dent and supreme. In these cities spiritual sustenance is bountifully provided, and incorruptible
delights have been ordained. The food they bestow
is the bread of heaven, and the Spirit they impart
is God's imperishable blessing. Upon detached
souls they bestow the gift of Unity, enrich the destitute, and offer the cup of knowledge unto them
who wander in the wilderness of ignorance. All
the guidance, the blessings, the learning, the understanding, the faith, and certitude, conferred
upon all that is in heaven and on earth, are hidden
and treasured within these Cities.

For instance, the Qur'án was an impregnable
stronghold unto the people of Muḥammad. In His
days, whosoever entered therein, was shielded
from the devilish assaults, the menacing darts, the
soul-devouring doubts, and blasphemous whisperings of the enemy. Upon him was also bestowed
a portion of the everlasting and goodly fruits—
the fruits of wisdom, from the divine Tree. To
him was given to drink the incorruptible waters
of the river of knowledge, and to taste the wine of
the mysteries of divine Unity.

All the things that people required in connection
with the Revelation of Muḥammad and His laws

were to be found revealed and manifest in that Riḍván of resplendent glory. That Book constitutes an abiding testimony to its people after Muḥammad, inasmuch as its decrees are indisputable, and its promise unfailing. All have been enjoined to follow the precepts of that Book until "the year sixty" [1]—the year of the advent of God's wondrous Manifestation. That Book is the Book which unfailingly leadeth the seeker unto the Riḍván of the divine Presence, and causeth him that hath forsaken his country and is treading the seeker's path to enter the Tabernacle of everlasting reunion. Its guidance can never err, its testimony no other testimony can excel. All other traditions, all other books and records, are bereft of such distinction, inasmuch as both the traditions and they that have spoken them are confirmed and proven solely by the text of that Book. Moreover, the traditions themselves grievously differ, and their obscurities are manifold.

Muḥammad, Himself, as the end of His mission drew nigh, spoke these words: "Verily, I leave amongst you My twin weighty testimonies: The Book of God and My Family." Although many

[1] The year 1260 A.H., the year of the Báb's Declaration.

traditions had been revealed by that Source of Prophethood and Mine of divine Guidance, yet He mentioned only that Book, thereby appointing it as the mightiest instrument and surest testimony for the seekers; a guide for the people until the Day of Resurrection.

With unswerving vision, with pure heart, and sanctified spirit, consider attentively what God hath established as the testimony of guidance for His people in His Book, which is recognized as authentic by both the high and lowly. To this testimony we both, as well as all the peoples of the world, must cling, that through its light we may know and distinguish between truth and falsehood, guidance and error. Inasmuch as Muḥammad hath confined His testimonies to His Book and to His Family, and whereas the latter hath passed away, there remaineth His Book only as His one testimony amongst the people.

In the beginning of His Book He saith: "Alif. Lám. Mím. No doubt is there about this Book: It is a guidance unto the God-fearing." [1] In the disconnected letters of the Qur'án the mysteries of the divine Essence are enshrined, and within their

[1] Qur'án 2 :1.

shells the pearls of His Unity are treasured. For lack of space We do not dwell upon them at this moment. Outwardly they signify Muḥammad Himself, Whom God addresseth saying: "O Muḥammad, there is no doubt nor uncertainty about this Book which hath been sent down from the heaven of divine Unity. In it is guidance unto them that fear God." Consider, how He hath appointed and decreed this self-same Book, the Qur'án, as a guidance unto all that are in heaven and on earth. He, the divine Being, and unknowable Essence, hath, Himself, testified that this Book is, beyond all doubt and uncertainty, the guide of all mankind until the Day of Resurrection. And now, We ask, is it fair for this people to view with doubt and misgiving this most weighty Testimony, the divine origin of which God hath proclaimed, and pronounced it to be the embodiment of truth? Is it fair for them to turn away from the thing which He hath appointed as the supreme Instrument of guidance for attainment unto the loftiest summits of knowledge, and to seek aught else but that Book? How can they allow men's absurd and foolish sayings to sow the seeds of distrust in their minds? How can they any longer idly contend that a certain person hath spoken this or that way, or that a certain thing did not come to pass? Had there been anything conceivable besides the Book of God which could prove a more potent instrument and a surer guide to mankind, would He have failed to reveal it in that verse?

It is incumbent upon us not to depart from God's irresistible injunction and fixed decree, as revealed in the above-mentioned verse. We should acknowledge the holy and wondrous Scriptures, for failing to do this we have failed to acknowledge the truth of this blessed verse. For it is evident that whoso hath failed to acknowledge the truth of the Qur'án hath in reality failed to acknowledge the truth of the preceding Scriptures. This is but the manifest implication of the verse. Were We to expound its inner meanings and unfold its hidden mysteries, eternity would never suffice to exhaust their import, nor would the universe be capable of hearing them! God verily testifieth to the truth of Our saying!

In another passage He likewise saith: "And if ye be in doubt as to that which We have sent down to Our Servant, then produce a Súrah like it, and summon your witnesses, beside God, if ye are men of truth." [1] Behold, how lofty is the station, and how consummate the virtue, of these verses which He hath declared to be His surest testimony, His infallible proof, the evidence of His all-subduing power, and a revelation of the potency of His will. He, the divine King, hath proclaimed the undisputed supremacy of the verses of His Book over all things that testify to His truth. For compared with all other proofs and tokens, the divinely-revealed verses shine as the sun, whilst all others are as stars. To the peoples of the world they are the abiding testimony, the incontrovertible proof, the shining light of the ideal King. Their excellence is unrivalled, their virtue nothing can surpass. They are the treasury of the divine pearls and the depository of the divine mysteries. They constitute the indissoluble Bond, the firm Cord, the 'Urvatu'l-Vuthqá, the inextinguishable Light. Through them floweth the river of divine knowledge, and gloweth the fire of His ancient and consummate wisdom. This is the fire which, in one and the same moment, kindleth the flame of love in the breasts of the faithful, and induceth the chill of heedlessness in the heart of the enemy.

O friend! It behooveth us not to waive the in-

[1] Qur'án 2:23.

junction of God, but rather acquiesce and submit
to that which He hath ordained as His divine Testimony. This verse is too weighty and pregnant an
utterance for this afflicted soul to demonstrate and
expound. God speaketh the truth and leadeth the
way. He, verily, is supreme over all His people;
He is the Mighty, the Beneficent.

Likewise, He saith: "Such are the verses of
God: with truth do We recite them to Thee. But
in what revelation will they believe, if they reject
God and His verses?" [1] If thou wilt grasp the implication of this verse, thou wilt recognize the
truth that no manifestation greater than the
Prophets of God hath ever been revealed, and no
testimony mightier than the testimony of their revealed verses hath ever appeared upon the
earth. Nay, this testimony no other testimony
can ever excel, except that which the Lord thy
God willeth.

In another passage He saith: "Woe to every
lying sinner, who heareth the verses of God recited
to him, and then, as though he heard them not,
persisteth in proud disdain! Apprise him of a

[1] Qur'án 45:5.

painful punishment." [1] The implications of this verse, alone, suffice all that is in heaven and on earth, were the people to ponder the verses of their Lord. For thou hearest how in this day the people disdainfully ignore the divinely-revealed verses, as though they were the meanest of all things. And yet, nothing greater than these verses hath ever appeared, nor will ever be made manifest in the world! Say unto them: "O heedless people! Ye repeat what your fathers, in a bygone age, have said. Whatever fruits they have gathered from the tree of their faithlessness, the same shall ye gather also. Ere long shall ye be gathered unto your fathers, and with them shall ye dwell in hellish fire. An ill abode! the abode of the people of tyranny."

In yet another passage He saith: "And when he becometh acquainted with any of Our verses he turneth them to ridicule. There is a shameful punishment for them!" [2] The people derisively observed saying: "Work thou another miracle, and give us another sign!" One would say: "Make now a part of the heaven to fall down upon us"; [3] and

[1] Qur'án 45:6.
[2] Qur'án 45:8.
[3] Qur'án 26:187.

another: "If this be the very truth from before Thee, rain down stones upon us from heaven."[1] Even as the people of Israel, in the time of Moses, bartered away the bread of heaven for the sordid things of the earth, these people, likewise, sought to exchange the divinely-revealed verses for their foul, their vile, and idle desires. In like manner, thou beholdest in this day that although spiritual sustenance hath descended from the heaven of divine mercy, and been showered from the clouds of His loving kindness, and although the seas of life, at the behest of the Lord of all being, are surging within the Riḍván of the heart, yet these people, ravenous as the dogs, have gathered around carrion, and contented themselves with the stagnant waters of a briny lake. Gracious God! how strange the way of this people! They clamour for guidance, although the standards of Him Who guideth all things are already hoisted. They cleave to the obscure intricacies of knowledge, when He, Who is the Object of all knowledge, shineth as the sun. They see the sun with their own eyes, and yet question that brilliant Orb as to the proof of its light. They behold the vernal showers descending upon them, and yet seek an evidence of that

[1] Qur'án 8:32.

bounty. The proof of the sun is the light thereof, which shineth and envelopeth all things. The evidence of the shower is the bounty thereof, which reneweth and investeth the world with the mantle of life. Yea, the blind can perceive naught from the sun except its heat, and the arid soil hath no share of the showers of mercy. "Marvel not if in the Qur'án the unbeliever perceiveth naught but the trace of letters, for in the sun, the blind findeth naught but heat."

In another passage He saith: "And when Our clear verses are recited to them, their only argument is to say, 'Bring back our fathers, if ye speak the truth!' "[1] Behold, what foolish evidences they sought from these Embodiments of an all-encompassing mercy! They scoffed at the verses, a single letter of which is greater than the creation of heavens and earth, and which quickeneth the dead of the valley of self and desire with the spirit of faith; and clamoured saying: "Cause our fathers to speed out of their sepulchres." Such was the perversity and pride of that people. Each one of these verses is unto all the peoples of the world an unfailing testimony and a glorious proof of His truth. Each of them verily sufficeth all mankind,

[1] Qur'án 45:24.

wert thou to meditate upon the verses of God. In the above-mentioned verse itself pearls of mysteries lie hidden. Whatever be the ailment, the remedy it offereth can never fail.

Heed not the idle contention of those who maintain that the Book and verses thereof can never be a testimony unto the common people, inasmuch as they neither grasp their meaning nor appreciate their value. And yet, the unfailing testimony of God to both the East and the West is none other than the Qur'án. Were it beyond the comprehension of men, how could it have been declared as a universal testimony unto all people? If their contention be true, none would therefore be required, nor would it be necessary for them to know God, inasmuch as the knowledge of the divine Being transcendeth the knowledge of His Book, and the common people would not possess the capacity to comprehend it.

Such contention is utterly fallacious and inadmissible. It is actuated solely by arrogance and pride. Its motive is to lead the people astray from the Riḍván of divine good-pleasure and to tighten the reins of their authority over the people. And yet, in the sight of God, these common people are infinitely superior and exalted above their religious leaders who have turned away from the one true God. The understanding of His words and the comprehension of the utterances of the Birds of Heaven are in no wise dependent upon human learning. They depend solely upon purity of heart, chastity of soul, and freedom of spirit. This is evidenced by those who, today, though without a single letter of the accepted standards of learning, are occupying the loftiest seats of knowledge; and the garden of their hearts is adorned, through the showers of divine grace, with the roses of wisdom and the tulips of understanding. Well is it with the sincere in heart for their share of the light of a mighty Day!

And likewise, He saith: "As for those who believe not in the verses of God, or that they shall ever meet Him, these of My mercy shall despair, and these doth a grievous chastisement await."[1] Also, "And they say, 'Shall we then abandon our gods for a crazed poet?' "[2] The implication of this verse is manifest. Behold what they observed after the verses were revealed. They called Him a poet, scoffed at the verses of God, and exclaimed say-

[1] Qur'án 29:23.
[2] Qur'án 37:36.

ing: "These words of his are but tales of the Ancients!" By this they meant that those words which were spoken by the peoples of old Muḥammad hath compiled and called them the Word of God.

Likewise, in this day, thou hast heard the people impute similar charges to this Revelation, saying: "He hath compiled these words from the words of old;" or "these words are spurious." Vain and haughty are their sayings, low their estate and station!

After the denials and denunciations which they uttered, and unto which We have referred, they protested saying: "No independent Prophet, according to our Scriptures, should arise after Moses and Jesus to abolish the Law of divine Revelation. Nay, he that is to be made manifest must needs fulfil the Law." Thereupon this verse, indicative of all the divine themes, and testifying to the truth that the flow of the grace of the All-Merciful can never cease, was revealed: "And Joseph came to you aforetime with clear tokens, but ye ceased not to doubt of the message with which He came to you, until, when He died, ye said, 'God will by no means raise up a Messenger after Him.' Thus God misleadeth him who is the transgressor the doubter." [1] Therefore, understand from this verse and know of a certainty that the people in every age, clinging to a verse of the Book, have uttered such vain and absurd sayings, contending that no Prophet should again be made manifest to the world. Even as the Christian divines who, holding fast to the verse of the Gospel to which We have already referred, have sought to explain that the law of the Gospel shall at no time be annulled, and that no independent Prophet shall again be made manifest, unless He confirmeth the law of the Gospel. Most of the people have become afflicted with the same spiritual disease.

Even as thou dost witness how the people of the Qur'án, like unto the people of old, have allowed the words "Seal of the Prophets" to veil their eyes. And yet, they themselves testify to this verse: "None knoweth the interpretation thereof but God and they that are well-grounded in knowledge." [2] And when He Who is well-grounded in all knowledge, He Who is the Mother, the Soul, the Secret, and the Essence thereof, revealeth that which is the least contrary to their desire, they bitterly oppose Him and shamelessly deny Him. These thou

[1] Qur'án 40:34.
[2] Qur'án 3:7.

[213]

hast already heard and witnessed. Such deeds and words have been solely instigated by leaders of religion, they that worship no God but their own desire, who bear allegiance to naught but gold, who are wrapt in the densest veils of learning, and who, enmeshed by its obscurities, are lost in the wilds of error. Even as the Lord of being hath explicitly declared: "What thinkest thou? He who hath made a God of his passions, and whom God causeth to err through a knowledge, and whose ears and whose heart He hath sealed up, and over whose sight He hath cast a veil—who, after his rejection by God, shall guide such a one? Will ye not then be warned?" [1]

Although the outward meaning of "Whom God causeth to err through a knowledge" is what hath been revealed, yet to Us it signifieth those divines of the age who have turned away from the Beauty of God, and who, clinging unto their own learning, as fashioned by their own fancies and desires, have denounced God's divine Message and Revelation. "Say: it is a weighty Message, from which ye turn aside!" [2] Likewise, He saith: "And when

[1] Qur'án 45:22.
[2] Qur'án 38:67.

Our clear verses are recited to them, they say, 'This is merely a man who would fain pervert you from your father's worship.' And they say, 'This is none other than a forged falsehood.'" [1]

Give ear unto God's holy Voice, and heed thou His sweet and immortal melody. Behold how He hath solemnly warned them that have repudiated the verses of God, and hath disowned them that have denied His holy words. Consider how far the people have strayed from the Kawthar of the divine Presence, and how grievous hath been the faithlessness and arrogance of the spiritually destitute in the face of that sanctified Beauty. Although that Essence of lovingkindness and bounty caused those evanescent beings to step into the realm of immortality, and guided those destitute souls to the sacred river of wealth, yet some denounced Him as "a calumniator of God, the Lord of all creatures," others accused Him of being "the one that withholdeth the people from the path of faith and true belief," and still others declared Him to be "a lunatic" and the like.

In like manner, thou observest in this day with what vile imputations they have assailed that Gem

[1] Qur'án 34:43.

of Immortality, and what unspeakable transgressions they have heaped upon Him Who is the Source of purity. Although God hath throughout His Book and in His holy and immortal Tablet warned them that deny and repudiate the revealed verses, and hath announced His grace unto them that accept them, yet behold the unnumbered cavils they raised against those verses which have been sent down from the new heaven of God's eternal holiness! This, notwithstanding the fact that no eye hath beheld so great an outpouring of bounty, nor hath any ear heard of such a revelation of lovingkindness. Such bounty and revelation have been made manifest, that the revealed verses seemed as vernal showers raining from the clouds of the mercy of the All-Bountiful. The Prophets "endowed with constancy," whose loftiness and glory shine as the sun, were each honoured with a Book which all have seen, and the verses of which have been duly ascertained. Whereas the verses which have rained from this Cloud of divine mercy have been so abundant that none hath yet been able to estimate their number. A score of volumes are now available. How many still remain beyond our reach! How many have been plundered and have fallen into the hands of the enemy, the fate of which none knoweth.

O brother, we should open our eyes, meditate upon His Word, and seek the sheltering shadow of the Manifestations of God, that perchance we may be warned by the unmistakable counsels of the Book, and give heed to the admonitions recorded in the holy Tablets; that we may not cavil at the Revealer of the verses, that we may resign ourselves wholly to His Cause, and embrace wholeheartedly His law, that haply we may enter the court of His mercy, and dwell upon the shore of His grace. He, verily, is merciful, and forgiving towards His servants.

And likewise, He saith: "Say, O people of the Book! do ye not disavow us only because we believe in God and in what He hath sent down to us, and in what He hath sent down aforetime, and because most of you are doers of ill?" [1] How explicitly doth this verse reveal Our purpose, and how clearly doth it demonstrate the truth of the testimony of the verses of God! This verse was revealed at a time when Islám was assailed by the infidels,

[1] Qur'án 5:62.

and its followers were accused of misbelief, when the Companions of Muḥammad were denounced as repudiators of God and as followers of a lying sorcerer. In its early days, when Islám was still to outward seeming devoid of authority and power, the friends of the Prophet, who had turned their face toward God, wherever they went, were harassed, persecuted, stoned and vilified. At such a time this blessed verse was sent down from the heaven of divine Revelation. It revealed an irrefutable evidence, and brought the light of an unfailing guidance. It instructed the companions of Muḥammad to declare the following unto the infidels and idolators: "Ye oppress and persecute us, and yet, what else have we done except that we have believed in God and in the verses sent down unto us through the tongue of Muḥammad, and in those which descended upon the Prophets of old?" By this is meant that their only guilt was to have recognized that the new and wondrous verses of God, which had descended upon Muḥammad, as well as those which had been revealed unto the Prophets of old, were all of God, and to have acknowledged and embraced their truth. This is the testimony which the divine King hath taught His servants.

In view of this, is it fair for this people to repudiate these newly-revealed verses which have encompassed both the East and the West, and to regard themselves as the upholders of true belief? Should they not rather believe in Him Who hath revealed these verses? Considering the testimony which He Himself hath established, how could He fail to account as true believers them that have testified to its truth? Far be it from Him that He should turn away from the gates of His mercy them that have turned unto and embraced the truth of the divine verses, or that He should threaten those that have clung to His sure testimony! He verily establisheth the truth through His verses, and confirmeth His Revelation by His words. He verily is the Powerful, the Help in peril, the Almighty.

And likewise, He saith: "And had We sent down unto Thee a Book written on parchment, and they had touched it with their hands, the infidels would surely have said 'This is naught but palpable sorcery.' " [1] Most of the verses of the Qur'án are indicative of this theme. We have, for the sake of brevity, mentioned only these verses. Consider,

[1] Qur'án 6:7.

hath anything else besides the verses been established in the whole Book, as a standard for the recognition of the Manifestations of His Beauty, that the people might cling to, and reject the Manifestations of God? On the contrary, in every instance, He hath threatened with fire those that repudiate and scoff at the verses, as already shown.

Therefore, should a person arise and bring forth a myriad verses, discourses, epistles, and prayers, none of which have been acquired through learning, what conceivable excuse could justify those that reject them, and deprive themselves of the potency of their grace? What answer could they give when once their soul hath ascended and departed from its gloomy temple? Could they seek to justify themselves by saying: "We have clung to a certain tradition, and not having beheld the literal fulfilment thereof, we have therefore raised such cavils against the Embodiments of divine Revelation, and kept remote from the law of God?" Hast thou not heard that among the reasons why certain Prophets have been designated as Prophets "endowed with constancy" was the revelation of a Book unto them? And yet, how could this people be justified in rejecting the Revealer and Author of so many volumes of verses, and follow the sayings of him who hath foolishly sown the seeds of doubt in the hearts of men, and who, Satan-like, hath risen to lead the people into the paths of perdition and error? How could they allow such things to deprive them of the light of the Sun of divine bounty? Aside from these things, if these people shun and reject such a divine Soul, such holy Breath, to whom, We wonder, could they cling, to whose face besides His Face could they turn? Yea—"All have a quarter of the Heavens to which they turn."[1] We have shown thee these two ways; walk thou the way thou choosest. This verily is the truth, and after truth there remaineth naught but error.

Amongst the proofs demonstrating the truth of this Revelation is this, that in every age and Dispensation, whenever the invisible Essence was revealed in the person of His Manifestation, certain souls, obscure and detached from all worldly entanglements, would seek illumination from the Sun of Prophethood and Moon of divine guidance, and would attain unto the divine Presence. For this

[1] Qur'án 2:148.

reason, the divines of the age and those possessed of wealth, would scorn and scoff at these people. Even as He hath revealed concerning them that erred: "Then said the chiefs of His people who believed not, 'We see in Thee but a man like ourselves; and we see not any who have followed Thee except our meanest ones of hasty judgment, nor see we any excellence in you above ourselves: nay, we deem you liars.'" [1] They caviled at those holy Manifestations, and protested saying: "None hath followed you except the abject amongst us, those who are worthy of no attention." Their aim was to show that no one amongst the learned, the wealthy, and the renowned believed in them. By this and similar proofs they sought to demonstrate the falsity of Him that speaketh naught but the truth.

In this most resplendent Dispensation, however, this most mighty Sovereignty, a number of illumined divines, of men of consummate learning, of doctors of mature wisdom, have attained unto His Court, drunk the cup of His divine Presence, and been invested with the honour of His most excellent favour. They have renounced, for the sake of the Beloved, the world and all that is therein. We

[1] Qur'án 11:27.   [222]

will mention the names of some of them, that perchance it may strengthen the faint-hearted, and encourage the timorous.

Among them was Mullá Ḥusayn, who became the recipient of the effulgent glory of the Sun of divine Revelation. But for him, God would not have been established upon the seat of His mercy, nor ascended the throne of eternal glory. Among them also was Siyyid Yaḥyá, that unique and peerless figure of his age,

Mullá Muḥammad 'Alíy-i-Zanjání
Mullá 'Alíy-i-Bastámí
Mullá Sa'íd-i-Bárfurúshí
Mullá Ni'matu'lláh-i-Mázindarání
Mullá Yúsuf-i-Ardibílí
Mullá Mihdíy-i-Khu'í
Siyyid Ḥusayn-i-Turshízí
Mullá Mihdíy-i-Kandí
Mullá Báqir
Mullá 'Abdu'l-Kháliq-i-Yazdí
Mullá 'Alíy-i-Baraqání

and others, well nigh four hundred in number, whose names are all inscribed upon the "Guarded Tablet" of God.

All these were guided by the light of that Sun of divine Revelation, confessed and acknowledged His truth. Such was their faith, that most of them renounced their substance and kindred, and cleaved to the good-pleasure of the All-Glorious. They laid down their lives for their Well-Beloved, and surrendered their all in His path. Their breasts were made targets for the darts of the enemy, and their heads adorned the spears of the infidel. No land remained which did not drink the blood of these embodiments of detachment, and no sword that did not bruise their necks. Their deeds, alone, testify to the truth of their words. Doth not the testimony of these holy souls, who have so gloriously risen to offer up their lives for their Beloved that the whole world marvelled at the manner of their sacrifice, suffice the people of this day? Is it not sufficient witness against the faithlessness of those who for a trifle betrayed their faith, who bartered away immortality for that which perisheth, who gave up the Kawthar of the divine Presence for salty springs, and whose one aim in life is to usurp the property of others? Even as thou dost witness how all of them have busied themselves with the vanities of the world, and have strayed far from Him Who is the Lord, the Most High.

Be fair: Is the testimony of those acceptable and worthy of attention whose deeds agree with their words, whose outward behaviour conforms with their inner life? The mind is bewildered at their deeds, and the soul marvelleth at their fortitude and bodily endurance. Or is the testimony of these faithless souls who breathe naught but the breath of selfish desire, and who lie imprisoned in the cage of their idle fancies, acceptable? Like the bats of darkness, they lift not their heads from their couch except to pursue the transient things of the world, and find no rest by night except as they labour to advance the aims of their sordid life. Immersed in their selfish schemes, they are oblivious of the divine Decree. In the day-time they strive with all their soul after worldly benefits, and in the night-season their sole occupation is to gratify their carnal desires. By what law or standard could men be justified in cleaving to the denials of such petty-minded souls, and in ignoring the faith of them that have renounced, for the sake of the good-pleasure of God, their life, and substance, their fame and renown, their reputation and honour?

Were not the happenings of the life of the "Prince of Martyrs"[1] regarded as the greatest of all events, as the supreme evidence of his truth?

[1] Imám Ḥusayn.

Did not the people of old declare those happenings to be unprecedented? Did they not maintain that no manifestation of truth hath ever evinced such constancy, such conspicuous glory? And yet, that episode of his life, commencing as it did in the morning, was brought to a close by the middle of the same day, whereas, these holy lights have, for eighteen years, heroically endured the showers of afflictions which, from every side, have rained upon them. With what love, what devotion, what exultation and holy rapture, they sacrificed their lives in the path of the All-Glorious! To the truth of this all witness. And yet, how can they belittle this Revelation? Hath any age witnessed such momentous happenings? If these companions be not the true strivers after God, who else could be called by this name? Have these companions been seekers after power or glory? Have they ever yearned for riches? Have they cherished any desire except the good-pleasure of God? If these companions, with all their marvellous testimonies and wondrous works, be false, who then is worthy to claim for himself the truth? I swear by God! Their very deeds are a sufficient testimony, and an irrefutable proof unto all the peoples of the earth, were men to ponder in their hearts the mysteries of divine Revelation. "And they who act unjustly shall soon know what lot awaiteth them!" [1]

Furthermore, the sign of truth and falsehood is designated and appointed in the Book. By this divinely-appointed touchstone, the claims and pretensions of all men must needs be assayed, so that the truthful may be known and distinguished from the imposter. This touchstone is no other than this verse: "Wish for death, if ye are men of truth." [2] Consider these martyrs of unquestionable sincerity, to whose truthfulness testifieth the explicit text of the Book, and all of whom, as thou hast witnessed, have sacrificed their life, their substance, their wives, their children, their all, and ascended unto the loftiest chambers of Paradise. Is it fair to reject the testimony of these detached and exalted beings to the truth of this pre-eminent and glorious Revelation and to regard as acceptable the denunciations which have been uttered against this resplendent Light by this faithless people, who for gold have forsaken their faith, and who for the sake of leadership have repudiated Him Who is the First Leader of all mankind? This,

[1] Qur'án 26:227.
[2] Qur'án 2:94, 62:6.

although their character is now revealed unto all people who have recognized them as those who will in no wise relinquish one jot or one tittle of their temporal authority for the sake of God's holy Faith, how much less their life, their substance, and the like.

Behold how the divine Touchstone hath, according to the explicit text of the Book, separated and distinguished the true from the false. Notwithstanding, they are still oblivious of this truth, and in the sleep of heedlessness, are pursuing the vanities of the world, and are occupied with thoughts of vain and earthly leadership.

"O Son of Man! Many a day hath passed over thee whilst thou hast busied thyself with thy fancies and idle imaginings. How long art thou to slumber on thy bed? Lift up thine head from slumber, for the Sun hath risen to the zenith; haply it may shine upon thee with the light of beauty."

Let it be known, however, that none of these doctors and divines to whom we have referred was invested with the rank and dignity of leadership. For well-known and influential leaders of religion, who occupy the seats of authority and exercise the functions of leadership, can in no wise bear allegiance to the Revealer of truth, except whomsoever thy Lord willeth. But for a few, such things have never come to pass. "And few of My servants are the thankful."[1] Even as in this Dispensation, not one amongst the renowned divines, in the grasp of whose authority were held the reins of the people, hath embraced the Faith. Nay, they have striven against it with such animosity and determination that no ear hath heard and no eye hath seen the like.

The Báb, the Lord, the most exalted—may the life of all be a sacrifice unto Him,—hath specifically revealed an Epistle unto the divines of every city, wherein He hath fully set forth the character of the denial and repudiation of each of them. "Wherefore, take ye good heed ye who are men of insight!"[2] By His references to their opposition He intended to invalidate the objections which the people of the Bayán might raise in the day of the manifestation of "Mustagháth,"[3] the day of the Latter Resurrection, claiming that, whereas in the Dispensation of the Bayán a number of divines

[1] Qur'án 34:13.
[2] Qur'án 59:2.
[3] He Who is invoked.

have embraced the Faith, in this latter Revelation none of these hath recognized His claim. His purpose was to warn the people lest, God forbid, they cling to such foolish thoughts and deprive themselves of the divine Beauty. Yea, these divines to whom We have referred, were mostly unrenowned, and, by the grace of God they were all purged of earthly vanities and free from the trappings of leadership. "Such is the bounty of God; to whom He will He giveth it."

Another proof and evidence of the truth of this Revelation, which amongst all other proofs shineth as the sun, is the constancy of the eternal Beauty in proclaiming the Faith of God. Though young and tender of age, and though the Cause He revealed was contrary to the desire of all the peoples of earth, both high and low, rich and poor, exalted and abased, king and subject, yet He arose and steadfastly proclaimed it. All have known and heard this. He was afraid of no one; He was regardless of consequences. Could such a thing be made manifest except through the power of a divine Revelation, and the potency of God's invincible Will? By the righteousness of God! Were any one to entertain so great a Revelation in his heart, the thought of such a declaration would alone confound him! Were the hearts of all men to be crowded into his heart, he would still hesitate to venture upon so awful an enterprise. He could achieve it only by the permission of God, only if the channel of his heart were to be linked with the Source of divine grace, and his soul be assured of the unfailing sustenance of the Almighty. To what, We wonder, do they ascribe so great a daring? Do they accuse Him of folly as they accused the Prophets of old? Or do they maintain that His motive was none other than leadership and the acquisition of earthly riches?

Gracious God! In His Book, which He hath entitled "Qayyúmu'l-Asmá',"—the first, the greatest and mightiest of all books—He prophesied His own martyrdom. In it is this passage: "O thou Remnant of God! I have sacrificed myself wholly for Thee; I have accepted curses for Thy sake; and have yearned for naught but martyrdom in the path of Thy love. Sufficient Witness unto me is God, the Exalted, the Protector, the Ancient of Days!"

Likewise, in His interpretation of the letter "Há," He craved martyrdom, saying: "Methinks

I heard a Voice calling in my inmost being: 'Do thou sacrifice the thing which Thou lovest most in the path of God, even as Ḥusayn, peace be upon him, hath offered up his life for My sake.' And were I not regardful of this inevitable mystery, by Him, Who hath my being between His hands even if all the kings of the earth were to be leagued together they would be powerless to take from me a single letter, how much less can these servants who are worthy of no attention, and who verily are of the outcast . . . That all may know the degree of My patience, My resignation, and self-sacrifice in the path of God."

Could the Revealer of such utterance be regarded as walking any way but the way of God, and as having yearned for aught else except His good-pleasure? In this very verse there lieth concealed a breath of detachment, which if it were to be breathed full upon the world, all beings would renounce their lives, and sacrifice their souls. Reflect upon the villainous behaviour of this generation, and witness their astounding ingratitude. Observe how they have closed their eyes to all this glory, and are abjectly pursuing those foul carcasses from whose bellies ascendeth the cry of the swallowed substance of the faithful. And yet, what unseemly calumnies they have hurled against those Daysprings of Holiness? Thus do We recount unto thee that which the hands of the infidels have wrought, they who, in the Day of Resurrection, have turned their face away from the divine Presence, whom God hath tormented with the fire of their own misbelief, and for whom He hath prepared in the world to come a chastise‧ment which shall devour both their bodies and souls. For these have said: "God is powerless, and His hand of mercy is fettered."

Steadfastness in the Faith is a sure testimony, and a glorious evidence of the truth. Even as the "Seal of the Prophets" hath said: "Two verses have made Me old." Both these verses are indicative of constancy in the Cause of God. Even as He saith: "Be thou steadfast as thou hast been bidden." [1]

And now consider how this Sadrih of the Riḍván of God hath, in the prime of youth, risen to proclaim the Cause of God. Behold what steadfastness that Beauty of God hath revealed. The whole world rose to hinder Him, yet it utterly

[1] Qur'án 11:113.

failed. The more severe the persecution they inflicted on that Sadrih of Blessedness, the more His fervour increased, and the brighter burned the flame of His love. All this is evident, and none disputeth its truth. Finally, He surrendered His soul, and winged His flight unto the realms above.

And among the evidences of the truth of His manifestation were the ascendancy, the transcendent power, and supremacy which He, the Revealer of being and Manifestation of the Adored, hath, unaided and alone, revealed throughout the world. No sooner had that eternal Beauty revealed Himself in Shíráz, in the year sixty, and rent asunder the veil of concealment, than the signs of the ascendancy, the might, the sovereignty, and power, emanating from that Essence of Essences and Sea of Seas, were manifest in every land. So much so, that from every city there appeared the signs, the evidences, the tokens, the testimonies of that divine Luminary. How many were those pure and kindly hearts which faithfully reflected the light of that eternal Sun, and how manifold the emanations of knowledge from that Ocean of divine wisdom which encompassed all beings! In every city, all the divines and dignitaries rose to hinder and repress them, and girded up the loins of malice, of envy, and tyranny for their suppression. How great the number of those holy souls, those essences of justice, who, accused of tyranny, were put to death! And how many embodiments of purity, who showed forth naught but true knowledge and stainless deeds, suffered an agonizing death! Notwithstanding all this, each of these holy beings, up to his last moment, breathed the Name of God, and soared in the realm of submission and resignation. Such was the potency and transmuting influence which He exercised over them, that they ceased to cherish any desire but His will, and wedded their soul to His remembrance.

Reflect: Who in this world is able to manifest such transcendent power, such pervading influence? All these stainless hearts and sanctified souls have, with absolute resignation, responded to the summons of His decree. Instead of complaining, they rendered thanks unto God, and amidst the darkness of their anguish they revealed naught but radiant acquiescence to His will. It is evident how relentless was the hate, and how bitter the malice and enmity entertained by all the peoples of the earth towards these companions. The persecution and pain they inflicted on these holy and spiritual beings were regarded by them as means unto salvation, prosperity, and everlasting success. Hath the world, since the days of Adam, witnessed such tumult, such violent commotion? Notwithstanding all the torture they suffered, and manifold the afflictions they endured, they became the object of universal opprobrium and execration. Methinks, patience was revealed only by virtue of their fortitude, and faithfulness itself was begotten only by their deeds.

Do thou ponder these momentous happenings in thy heart, so that thou mayest apprehend the greatness of this Revelation, and perceive its stupendous glory. Then shall the spirit of faith, through the grace of the Merciful, be breathed into thy being, and thou shalt be established and abide upon the seat of certitude. The one God is My witness! Wert thou to ponder a while, thou wilt recognize that, apart from all these established truths and above-mentioned evidences, the repudiation, cursing, and execration, pronounced by the people of the earth, are in themselves the mightiest proof and the surest testimony of the truth of these heroes of the field of resignation and detachment. Whenever thou dost meditate upon the cavils uttered by all the people, be they divines, learned or ignorant, the firmer and the more steadfast wilt thou grow in the Faith. For whatsoever hath come to pass, hath been prophesied by them who are the Mines of divine knowledge, and Recipients of God's eternal law.

Although We did not intend to make mention of the traditions of a bygone age, yet, because of Our love for thee, We will cite a few which are applicable to Our argument. We do not feel their necessity, however, inasmuch as the things We have already mentioned suffice the world and all that is therein. In fact, all the Scriptures and the mysteries thereof are condensed into this brief account. So much so, that were a person to ponder it a while in his heart, he would discover from all that hath been said the mysteries of the Words of God, and would apprehend the meaning of whatever hath been manifested by that ideal King. As the people differ in their understanding and station, We will accordingly make mention of a few traditions, that these may impart constancy to the wavering soul, and tranquillity to the troubled mind. Thereby, will the testimony of God unto the people, both high and low, be complete and perfect.

Among them is the tradition, "And when the Standard of Truth is made manifest, the people of both the East and the West curse it." The wine of renunciation must needs be quaffed, the lofty heights of detachment must needs be attained, and the meditation referred to in the words "One hour's reflection is preferable to seventy years of pious worship" must needs be observed, so that the secret of the wretched behaviour of the people might be discovered, those people who, despite the love and yearning for truth which they profess, curse the followers of Truth when once He hath been made manifest. To this truth the above-mentioned tradition beareth witness. It is evident that the reason for such behaviour is none other than the annulment of those rules, customs, habits, and ceremonials to which they have been subjected. Otherwise, were the Beauty of the Merciful to comply with those same rules and customs, which are current amongst the people, and were He to sanction their observances, such conflict and mischief would in no wise be made manifest in the world. This exalted tradition is attested and sub-

stantiated by these words which He hath revealed:
"The day when the Summoner shall summon to a
stern business." [1]

The divine call of the celestial Herald from beyond the Veil of Glory, summoning mankind to
renounce utterly all the things to which they
cleave, is repugnant to their desire; and this is
the cause of the bitter trials and violent commo-
tions which have occurred. Consider the way of the
people. They ignore these well-founded traditions,
all of which have been fulfilled, and cling unto
those of doubtful validity, and ask why these have
not been fulfilled. And yet, those things which to
them were inconceivable have been made manifest.
The signs and tokens of the Truth shine even as
the midday sun, and yet the people are wandering,
aimlessly and perplexedly, in the wilderness of
ignorance and folly. Notwithstanding all the verses
of the Qur'án, and the recognized traditions,
which are all indicative of a new Faith, a new
Law, and a new Revelation, this generation still
waiteth in expectation of beholding the promised
One who should uphold the Law of the Muḥammadan Dispensation. The Jews and the

[1] Qur'án 54:6.

Christians in like manner uphold the same contention.

Among the utterances that foreshadow a new Law and a new Revelation are the passages in the "Prayer of Nudbih": "Where is He Who is preserved to renew the ordinances and laws? Where is He Who hath the authority to transform the Faith and the followers thereof?" He hath, likewise, revealed in the Zíyárat: [1] "Peace be upon the Truth made new." Abú-'Abdi'lláh, questioned concerning the character of the Mihdí, answered saying: "He will perform that which Muḥammad, the Messenger of God, hath performed, and will demolish whatever hath been before Him even as the Messenger of God hath demolished the ways of those that preceded Him."

Behold, how, notwithstanding these and similar traditions, they idly contend that the laws formerly revealed, must in no wise be altered. And yet, is not the object of every Revelation to effect a transformation in the whole character of mankind, a transformation that shall manifest itself both outwardly and inwardly, that shall affect both its inner life and external conditions? For if the char-

[1] Visiting Tablet revealed by 'Alí.

acter of mankind be not changed, the futility of God's universal Manifestations would be apparent. In the "'Aválim," an authoritative and well-known book, it is recorded: "A Youth from Baní-Háshim shall be made manifest, Who will reveal a new Book and promulgate a new law;" then follow these words: "Most of His enemies will be the divines." In another passage, it is related of Ṣádiq, son of Muḥammad, that he spoke the following: "There shall appear a Youth from Baní-Háshim, Who will bid the people plight fealty unto Him. His Book will be a new Book, unto which He shall summon the people to pledge their faith. Stern is His Revelation unto the Arab. If ye hear about Him, hasten unto Him." How well have they followed the directions of the Imáms of the Faith and Lamps of certitude! Although it is clearly stated: "Were ye to hear that a Youth from Baní-Háshim hath appeared, summoning the people unto a new and Divine Book, and to new and Divine laws, hasten unto Him," yet have they all declared that Lord of being an infidel, and pronounced Him a heretic. They hastened not unto that Háshimite Light, that divine Manifestation, except with drawn swords, and hearts filled with malice. Moreover, observe how explicitly the enmity of the divines hath been mentioned in the books. Notwithstanding all these evident and significant traditions, all these unmistakable and undisputed allusions, the people have rejected the immaculate Essence of knowledge and of holy utterance, and have turned unto the exponents of rebellion and error. Despite these recorded traditions and revealed utterances, they speak only that which is prompted by their own selfish desires. And should the Essence of Truth reveal that which is contrary to their inclinations and desires, they will straightway denounce Him as an infidel, and will protest saying: "This is contrary to the sayings of the Imáms of the Faith and of the resplendent lights. No such thing hath been provided by our inviolable Law." Even so in this day such worthless statements have been and are being made by these poor mortals.

And now, consider this other tradition, and observe how all these things have been foretold. In "Arba'ín" it is recorded: "Out of Baní-Háshim there shall come forth a Youth Who shall reveal new laws. He shall summon the people unto Him, but none will heed His call. Most of His enemies will be the divines. His bidding they will not obey, but will protest saying: 'This is contrary to that which hath been handed down unto us by the Imáms of the Faith.'" In this day, all are repeating these very same words, utterly unaware that He is established upon the throne of "He doeth whatsoever He willeth," and abideth upon the seat of "He ordaineth whatsoever He pleaseth."

No understanding can grasp the nature of His Revelation, nor can any knowledge comprehend the full measure of His Faith. All sayings are dependent upon His sanction, and all things stand in need of His Cause. All else save Him are created by His command, and move and have their being through His law. He is the Revealer of the divine mysteries, and the Expounder of the hidden and ancient wisdom. Thus it is related in the "Biháru'l-Anvár," the "'Aválim," and the "Yanbú'" of Ṣádiq, son of Muḥammad, that he spoke these words: "Knowledge is twenty and seven letters. All that the Prophets have revealed are two letters thereof. No man thus far hath known more than these two letters. But when the Qá'im shall arise, He will cause the remaining twenty and five letters to be made manifest." Consider; He hath declared Knowledge to consist of twenty and seven letters, and regarded all the Prophets, from Adam even unto the "Seal," as Expounders of only two letters thereof and of having been sent down with these two letters. He also saith that the Qá'im will reveal all the remaining twenty and five letters. Behold from this utterance how great and lofty is His station! His rank excelleth that of all the Prophets, and His Revelation transcendeth the comprehension and understanding of all their chosen ones. A Revelation, of which the Prophets of God, His saints and chosen ones, have either not been informed, or which, in pursuance of God's inscrutable Decree, they have not disclosed,—such a Revelation these mean and depraved people have sought to measure with their own deficient minds, their own deficient learning and understanding. Should it fail to conform to their standards, they straightway reject it. "Thinkest thou that the greater part of them hear or understand? They are even like unto the brutes! yea, they stray even further from the path!" [1]

How, We wonder, do they explain the afore-mentioned tradition, a tradition which, in unmis-takable terms, foreshadoweth the revelation of

[1] Qur'án 25:44.

things inscrutable, and the occurrence of new and wondrous events in His day? Such marvellous happenings kindle so great a strife amongst the people, that all the divines and doctors sentence Him and His companions to death, and all the peoples of the earth arise to oppose Him. Even as it hath been recorded in the "Káfí," in the tradition of Jábir, in the "Tablet of Fáṭimih," concerning the character of the Qá'im: "He shall manifest the perfection of Moses, the splendour of Jesus, and the patience of Job. His chosen ones shall be abased in His day. Their heads shall be offered as presents even as the heads of the Turks and the Daylamites. They shall be slain and burnt. Fear shall seize them; dismay and alarm shall strike terror into their hearts. The earth shall be dyed with their blood. Their womenfolk shall bewail and lament. These indeed are my friends!" Consider, not a single letter of this tradition hath remained unfulfilled. In most of the places their blessed blood hath been shed; in every city they have been made captives, have been paraded throughout the provinces, and some have been burnt with fire. And yet no one hath paused to reflect that if the promised Qá'im should reveal the law and ordinances of a former Dispensation, why then should such traditions have been recorded, and why should there arise such a degree of strife and conflict that the people should regard the slaying of these companions as an obligation imposed upon them, and deem the persecution of these holy souls as a means of attaining unto the highest favour?

Moreover, observe how these things that have come to pass, and the acts which have been perpetrated, have all been mentioned in former traditions. Even as it hath been recorded in the "Rawḍiy-i-Káfí," concerning "Zawrá'." In the "Rawḍiy-i-Káfí" it is related of Mu'áviyih, son of Vahháb, that Abú-'Abdi'lláh hath spoken: "Knowest thou Zawrá?" I said: "May my life be a sacrifice unto thee! They say it is Baghdád." "Nay," he answered. And then added: "Hast thou entered the city of Rayy?",[1] to which I made reply: "Yea, I have entered it." Whereupon, He enquired: "Didst thou visit the cattle-market?" "Yea," I answered. He said: "Hast thou seen the black mountain on the right hand side of the road? The same is Zawrá'. There shall eighty men, of the children of certain ones, be slain, all of whom

[1] Ancient city near which Ṭihrán is built.

are worthy to be called caliphs." "Who will slay them?" I asked. He made reply: "The children of Persia!"

Such is the condition and fate of His companions which in former days hath been foretold. And now observe how, according to this tradition, Zawrá' is no other but the land of Rayy. In that place His companions have been with great suffering put to death, and all these holy beings have suffered martyrdom at the hand of the Persians, as recorded in the tradition. This thou hast heard, and unto it all testify. Wherefore, then, do not these grovelling, worm-like men pause to meditate upon these traditions, all of which are manifest as the sun in its noon-tide glory? For what reason do they refuse to embrace the Truth, and allow certain traditions, the significance of which they have failed to grasp, to withhold them from the recognition of the Revelation of God and His Beauty, and to cause them to dwell in the infernal abyss? Such things are to be attributed to naught but the faithlessness of the divines and doctors of the age. Of these, Ṣádiq, son of Muḥammad, hath said: "The religious doctors of that age shall be the most wicked of the divines beneath the shadow of heaven. Out of them hath mischief proceeded, and unto them it shall return."

We entreat the learned men of the Bayán not to follow in such ways, not to inflict, at the time of Mustagháth, upon Him Who is the divine Essence, the heavenly Light, the absolute Eternity, the Beginning and the End of the Manifestations of the Invisible, that which hath been inflicted in this day. We beg them not to depend upon their intellect, their comprehension and learning, nor to contend with the Revealer of celestial and infinite knowledge. And yet, notwithstanding all these admonitions, We perceive that a one-eyed man, who himself is the chief of the people, is arising with the utmost malevolence against Us. We foresee that in every city people will arise to suppress the Blessed Beauty, that the companions of that Lord of being and ultimate Desire of all men will flee from the face of the oppressor and seek refuge from him in the wilderness, whilst others will resign themselves and, with absolute detachment, will sacrifice their lives in His path. Methinks We can discern one who is reputed for such devoutness and piety that men deem it an obligation to obey him, and to whose command they consider it necessary to submit, who will arise to assail the very root of the divine Tree, and endeavour to the uttermost of his power to resist and oppose Him. Such is the way of the people!

We fain would hope that the people of the Bayán will be enlightened, will soar in the realm of the spirit and abide therein, will discern the Truth, and recognize with the eye of insight dissembling falsehood. In these days, however, such odours of jealousy are diffused, that—I swear by the Educator of all beings, visible and invisible—from the beginning of the foundation of the world—though it hath no beginning—until the present day, such malice, envy, and hate have in no wise appeared, nor will they ever be witnessed in the future. For a number of people who have never inhaled the fragrance of justice, have raised the standard of sedition, and have leagued themselves against Us. On every side We witness the menace of their spears, and in all directions We recognize the shafts of their arrows. This, although We have never gloried in any thing, nor did We seek preference over any soul. To everyone We have been a most kindly companion, a most forbearing and affectionate friend. In the company of the poor We have sought their fellowship, and amidst the exalted and learned We have been submissive and resigned. I swear by God, the one true God! grievous as have been the woes and sufferings which the hand of the enemy and the people of the Book inflicted upon Us, yet all these fade into utter nothingness when compared with that which hath befallen Us at the hand of those who profess to be Our friends.

What more shall We say? The universe, were it to gaze with the eye of justice, would be incapable of bearing the weight of this utterance! In the early days of Our arrival in this land, when We discerned the signs of impending events, We decided, ere they happened, to retire. We betook Ourselves to the wilderness, and there, separated and alone, led for two years a life of complete solitude. From Our eyes there rained tears of anguish, and in Our bleeding heart there surged an ocean of agonizing pain. Many a night We had no food for sustenance, and many a day Our body found no rest. By Him Who hath My being between His hands! notwithstanding these showers of afflictions and unceasing calamities, Our soul was wrapt in blissful joy, and Our whole being evinced an ineffable gladness. For in Our solitude We were unaware of the harm or benefit, the health or ailment, of any soul. Alone, We communed with Our spirit, oblivious of the world and all that is therein. We knew not, however, that the mesh of divine destiny exceedeth the vastest of mortal conceptions, and the dart of His decree transcendeth the boldest of human designs. None can escape the snares He setteth, and no soul can find release except through submission to His will. By the righteousness of God! Our withdrawal contemplated no return, and Our separation hoped for no reunion. The one object of Our retirement was to avoid becoming a subject of discord among the faithful, a source of disturbance unto Our companions, the means of injury to any soul, or the cause of sorrow to any heart. Beyond these, We cherished no other intention, and apart from them, We had no end in view. And yet, each person schemed after his own desire, and pursued his own idle fancy, until the hour when, from the Mystic Source, there came the summons bidding Us return whence We came. Surrendering Our will to His, We submitted to His injunction.

What pen can recount the things We beheld upon Our return! Two years have elapsed during

which Our enemies have ceaselessly and assidu-
ously contrived to exterminate Us, whereunto all
witness. Nevertheless, none amongst the faithful
hath risen to render Us any assistance, nor did any
one feel inclined to help in Our deliverance. Nay,
instead of assisting Us, what showers of continu-
ous sorrows, their words and deeds have caused to
rain upon Our soul! Amidst them all, We stand,
life in hand, wholly resigned to His will; that
perchance, through God's loving kindness and His
grace, this revealed and manifest Letter may lay
down His life as a sacrifice in the path of the
Primal Point, the most exalted Word. By Him at
Whose bidding the Spirit hath spoken, but for this
yearning of Our soul, We would not, for one moment, have tarried any longer in this city. "Sufficient Witness is God unto Us." We conclude Our
argument with the words: "There is no power nor
strength but in God alone." "We are God's, and to
Him shall we return."

They that have hearts to understand, they that
have quaffed the Wine of love, who have not for
one moment gratified their selfish desires, will behold, resplendent as the sun in its noon-tide glory,
those tokens, testimonies, and evidences that attest
the truth of this wondrous Revelation, this tran-

scendent and divine Faith. Reflect, how the people have rejected the Beauty of God, and have clung unto their covetous desires. Notwithstanding all these consummate verses, these unmistakable allusions, which have been revealed in the "Most weighty Revelation," the Trust of God amongst men, and despite these evident traditions, each more manifest than the most explicit utterance, the people have ignored and repudiated their truth, and have held fast to the letter of certain traditions which, according to their understanding, they have found inconsistent with their expectations, and the meaning of which they have failed to grasp. They have thus shattered every hope, and deprived themselves of the pure wine of the All-Glorious, and the clear and incorruptible waters of the immortal Beauty.

Consider, that even the year in which that Quintessence of Light is to be made manifest hath been specifically recorded in the traditions, yet they still remain unmindful, nor do they for one moment cease to pursue their selfish desires. According to the tradition, Mufaḍḍal asked Ṣádiq saying: "What of the sign of His manifestation, O my master?" He made reply: "In the year sixty,

His Cause shall be made manifest, and His Name shall be proclaimed."

How strange! Notwithstanding these explicit and manifest references these people have shunned the Truth. For instance, mention of the sorrows, the imprisonment and afflictions inflicted upon that Essence of divine virtue hath been made in the former traditions. In the "Biḥár" it is recorded: "In our Qá'im there shall be four signs from four Prophets, Moses, Jesus, Joseph, and Muḥammad. The sign from Moses, is fear and expectation; from Jesus, that which was spoken of Him; from Joseph, imprisonment and dissimulation; from Muḥammad, the revelation of a Book similar to the Qur'án." Notwithstanding such a conclusive tradition, which in such unmistakable language hath foreshadowed the happenings of the present day, none hath been found to heed its prophecy, and methinks none will do so in the future, except him whom thy Lord willeth. "God indeed shall make whom He will to hearken, but We shall not make those who are in their graves to hearken."

It is evident unto thee that the Birds of Heaven and Doves of Eternity speak a twofold language. One language, the outward language, is devoid of allusions, is unconcealed and unveiled; that it may be a guiding lamp and a beaconing light whereby wayfarers may attain the heights of holiness, and seekers may advance into the realm of eternal reunion. Such are the unveiled traditions and the evident verses already mentioned. The other language is veiled and concealed, so that whatever lieth hidden in the heart of the malevolent may be made manifest and their innermost being be disclosed. Thus hath Ṣádiq, son of Muḥammad, spoken: "God verily will test them and sift them." This is the divine standard, this is the Touchstone of God, wherewith He proveth His servants. None apprehendeth the meaning of these utterances except them whose hearts are assured, whose souls have found favour with God, and whose minds are detached from all else but Him. In such utterances, the literal meaning, as generally understood by the people, is not what hath been intended. Thus it is recorded: "Every knowledge hath seventy meanings, of which one only is known amongst the people. And when the Qá'im shall arise, He shall reveal unto men all that which remaineth." He also saith: "We speak one word, and by it we intend one and seventy meanings; each one of these meanings we can explain."

These things We mention only that the people may not be dismayed because of certain traditions and utterances, which have not yet been literally fulfilled, that they may rather attribute their perplexity to their own lack of understanding, and not to the non-fulfilment of the promises in the traditions, inasmuch as the meaning intended by the Imáms of the Faith is not known by this people, as evidenced by the traditions themselves. The people, therefore, must not allow such utterances to deprive them of the divine bounties, but should rather seek enlightenment from them who are the recognized Expounders thereof, so that the hidden mysteries may be unravelled, and be made manifest unto them.

We perceive none, however, amongst the people of the earth who, sincerely yearning for the Truth, seeketh the guidance of the divine Manifestations concerning the abstruse matters of his Faith. All are dwellers in the land of oblivion, and all are followers of the people of wickedness and rebellion. God will verily do unto them that which they themselves are doing, and will forget them even as they have ignored His Presence in His day. Such is His decree unto those that have denied Him, and such will it be unto them that have rejected His signs.

We conclude Our argument with His words—exalted is He—"And whoso shall withdraw from the remembrance of the Merciful, We will chain a Satan unto him, and he shall be his fast companion." [1] "And whoso turneth away from My remembrance, truly his shall be a life of misery." [2]

Thus hath it been revealed aforetime, were ye to comprehend.

Revealed by the "Bá' " and the "Há'." [3]

Peace be upon him that inclineth his ear unto the melody of the Mystic Bird calling from the Sadratu'l-Muntahá!

Glorified be our Lord, the Most High!

[1] Qur'án 43:36.
[2] Qur'án 20:124.
[3] B and H meaning Bahá.

END

GLOSSARY AND NOTES

'Abdu'lláh: The father of the Prophet. He belonged to the family of Háshim, the noblest tribe of the Quraish section of the Arabian race, directly descended from Ishmael.

'Abdu'lláh-i-Ubayy: A prominent opponent of Muḥammad; called "the prince of hypocrites."

Abraham: See Genesis 11–25; *Some Answered Questions,* pp. 14–16. Scholars give 2100 B.C.–2000 B.C. as his dates. Regarded by Jews, Christians, and Muslims as the Friend of God, the Father of the Faithful.

Abú-'Abdi'lláh: Designation of the sixth Imám, Ja'far-i-Ṣádiq (the Veridical), great-grandson of al-Ḥusayn. Died A.D. 765, poisoned by Manṣúr, the 'Abbáside Caliph.

Abú'Amír: An opponent of Muḥammad; a monk.

Abú-Jahl: Literally, "the Father of Folly"; so styled by the Muslims. An implacable enemy of the Prophet.

'Alí: The son-in-law of the Prophet, the first of the twelve Imáms.

Alif. Lám. Mím.: These and other disconnected letters appear at the head of twenty-nine súrihs of the Qur'án.

Al-Medina: Literally, "the city," so called as giving shelter to Muḥammad: formerly Yathrib. The burial place of Muḥammad; second only to Mecca in sanctity.

Amalekites: Expelled in early times from Babylonia, they spread through Arabia to Palestine and Syria and as far as Egypt, to which they gave several of its Pharaohs.

Athím: Sinner.

'Aválim: A compilation of Shí'ih traditions.

Báb: The Qá'im and Mihdí of Islám, and the Forerunner of Bahá'u'lláh. (Birth of the Báb: October 20, 1819; His Martyrdom: July 9, 1850).

GLOSSARY AND NOTES

Baghdád: Founded by the Caliph at Mansur in A.D. 762 on the site of a Christian village on the western bank of the Tigris. It remained for 500 years the seat of the Abbasid Government.

Bahá: Literally, "Glory," "Splendor," referring to Bahá'u'-lláh (Mírzá Ḥusayn 'Alí) who had not yet declared Himself but had been already designated by this title.

Bahá'u'lláh: The Founder of the Bahá'í Faith, the title being recorded in the Persian Bayán of the Báb and meaning the Glory, the Light, and the Splendor of God. (Birth of Bahá'u'lláh: November 12, 1817; His death: May 29, 1892).

Baní-Háshim: The family to which Muḥammad belonged.

Baṭḥá: Mecca.

Bayán: The Bayán (Exposition) is the chief doctrinal work of the Báb. It is described in *God Passes By* (pp. 24–25) as a "monumental repository of the laws and precepts of the new Dispensation and the treasury enshrining most of the Báb's references and tributes to, as well as His warning regarding, *'Him Whom God will make manifest'*. . . . this Book, of about eight thousand verses, occupying a pivotal position in Bábí literature, should be regarded primarily as a eulogy of the Promised One rather than a code of laws and ordinances designed to be a permanent guide to future generations." The Báb also wrote "the smaller and less weighty Arabic Bayán."

Biḥár: Reference to Shí'ih tradition.

Biḥáru'l-Anvár: A compilation of Shí'ih traditions.

Caiaphas: The Jewish high priest who presided at the court which tried and condemned Jesus.

Cain and Abel: The two sons of Adam and Eve. See Genesis 4 and Qur'án, súrih 5.

Caliphs: Literally, "successors" or "vicegerents." The Shí'ihs hold that the successors of the Prophet must be the members of His own family, but they do not use the title <u>Kh</u>alífih or "Caliph." The Sultán of Turkey assumed this title early in the 16th century.

Cherubim: In the Bible the Cherubim appear as distinct from the angels who are Jehovah's messengers, while the Cherubim are found where God is personally present: e.g. "And he [God] rode upon a cherub." (Psalms 18: 10). Figures of Cherubim were wrought into the hangings of the Holy of Holies and were represented above the Mercy Seat within. In later tradition, the Cherubim were included among the nine orders of angels.

Copt: The Copts were descendants of the ancient Egyptian stock. They were unbelievers in the time of Moses. The Septs were the tribes of Israel.

Crimson Pillar: An allusion to the Religion of Bahá'u'lláh, crimsoned with the blood of martyrs.

Divine Elixir: Symbolic reference to the Elixir of the alchemists, that was supposed to transform base metals into gold.

Fátimih: The daughter of Muḥammad and <u>Kh</u>adíjih. She married 'Alí, the cousin of Muḥammad, and had three sons. One died in infancy and from the other two, Ḥasan and Ḥusayn, are descended the posterity of the Prophet known as Siyyids.

Gabriel: The highest of all the angels, the Holy Spirit. It is his duty to write down the decrees of God; through him the Qur'án was revealed to Muḥammad.

Há: The letter H, the number of which is 5, and which is sometimes used as a symbol of Bahá'u'lláh: see *Four Valleys,* p. 56 n.

Hájí Mírzá Karím <u>Kh</u>án: A pretender to knowledge, author of a book "Guidance to the Ignorant" ("Ir<u>sh</u>ádu'l-'Avám"), whose works perished with him.

GLOSSARY AND NOTES

Hamzih: "Prince of Martyrs," the title given to Muḥammad's uncle.

Herod: Herod I ("The Great"). An Idumaean by race, but brought up a Jew. He was appointed by the Roman Senate in 40 B.C. as King of Judea. He rebuilt the Temple in Jerusalem.

Ḥijáz: A region in southwestern Arabia which may be considered the holy land of the Muslims since it contains the sacred cities of Medina and Mecca and many other places connected with the history of Muḥammad. The "language of Ḥijáz" is Arabic.

Húd: A prophet sent to the tribe of 'Ád. He was descended from Noah and is referred to in the Qur'án in súrih 7:63–70; súrih 11:52–63; and in súrih 26:123–139.

Ḥusayn: The third Imám. Son of 'Alí and Fáṭimih.

Ibn-i-Ṣúríyá: A learned Jewish Rabbi at the time of Muḥammad.

Imám 'Alí: The cousin and first disciple of Muḥammad; husband of Muḥammad's daughter, Fáṭimih; and through his son Ḥusayn, ancestor of Siyyid 'Alí Muḥammad, the Báb.

'Imrán: The father of Moses and Aaron; Qur'án, súrih 3:30 and Bible, Exodus 6:20.

'Iráq: Part of the Turkish Empire in 1862 when this book was revealed. Now an Arab Kingdom with Baghdád as its capital.

Joseph: The son of Jacob, and in the Qur'án an inspired prophet.

Ka'b-Ibn-i-Ashraf: Conspired with the Prophet's arch-enemy, Abú Ṣufyán, to compass the Prophet's death.

Ka'bih: Literally, a "cube." The cube-like building in

the center of the Mosque at Mecca, which contains the Black Stone.

Káfí: An important collection of Shí'ih traditions, Jábir being the authority for the quotation given on p. 245.

Karbilá: A city about 55 miles southwest of Baghdád on the Euphrates.

Karim: Honorable.

Kawthar: A river of Paradise from which all the others flow. Part of its waters are led into a great lake on the shores of which the souls of the faithful rest when they have crossed the terrible bridge which is laid over the midst of Hell.

Khaybar: The name of a famous oasis, and of its principal settlement, near Medina, where significant events in the ministry of Muḥammad took place.

Kúfih: A city on the west bank of the Euphrates, which has now entirely disappeared.

Letters of Unity: Apostles of the Prophet.

Leviathan: An unidentified aquatic monster; whale or serpent.

Magi: A caste of priests and sages among the ancient Persians.

Manifestation: The nature of a prophet or the Manifestation of God is thus described in *Gleanings from the Writings of Bahá'u'lláh* (pp. 66–67): ". . . since there can be no tie of direct intercourse to bind the one true God with His creation, and no resemblance whatever can exist between the transient and the Eternal, the contingent and the Absolute, He hath ordained that in every age and dispensation a pure and stainless Soul be made manifest in the kingdoms of earth and heaven. . . . These Essences of Detachment, these resplendent Realities are the channels of God's all-pervasive grace. Led by the light of unfailing guidance, and invested with supreme sovereignty, they are commissioned to use the

GLOSSARY AND NOTES

inspiration of Their words, the effusions of Their infallible grace and the sanctifying breezes of Their Revelation for the cleansing of every longing heart and receptive spirit from the dross and dust of earthly cares and limitations."

Mecca: The capital of Arabia, the birthplace of Muḥammad, the site of the Ka'bih, and the most sacred city of Islám.

Midian: A city and district on the Red Sea, southeast of Mt. Sinai, occupied by the descendants of Midian, son of Abraham and Keturah. Qur'án, súrih 7:83.

"Mi'ráj": The night journey of Muḥammad with Gabriel.

Moses: One of the six great prophets, according to the Muḥammadans. See Exodus 4:16, where God says to Moses: "thou shalt be to him instead of God"; and Exodus 7:1: "I have made thee a god to Pharaoh." Moses led the exodus from Egypt, which is now dated about 1440 B.C.

Mufaḍḍal: Reference to Shí'ih tradition.

Muḥammad: The Prophet of Islám and Revealer of the Qur'án. Born August A.D. 570. Declared His Mission A.D. 613. Fled to Medina A.D. 622. See *Some Answered Questions,* pp. 22–29. Foretold by Moses, Deut. 18:15; by St. John the Divine, Rev. 11 (see *Some Answered Questions,* p. 53 ff.).

Mullá 'Abdu'l-Kháliq-i-Yazdí: At first a Jewish priest, he accepted Islám, joined the Shaykhí School and was converted by Mullá Ḥusayn to the Bábí Faith.

Mullá 'Alíy-i-Baraqání: Uncle of Ṭáhirih, one of the most learned and famous members of the Shaykhí community. Being converted to the Bábí Faith, he became in Ṭihrán one of its most earnest and able expositors.

Mullá 'Alíy-i-Bastámí: One of the Letters of the Living. Sent on a special mission by the Báb from Shíráz in 1844, he became the first to suffer and to lay down his life in the path of this new Faith.

GLOSSARY AND NOTES

Mullá Báqir: A brother of Mullá Mihdíy-i-Kandí, martyred at Ṭabarsí.

Mullá Ḥusayn: The first to believe in the Báb, the first "Letter of the Living," the "Bábu'l-Báb"—meaning "the Gate of the Gate," a title given him by the Báb. Born in 1813, he was for nine years a student of Siyyid Káẓim and for five a follower of the Báb. He was martyred at the fort of S͟haykh Ṭabarsí, on February 2, 1849.

Mullá Mihdíy-i-K͟hu'í: A close companion of Bahá'u'lláh and tutor to the children of His household. Martyred at Ṭabarsí.

Mullá Muḥammad-'Alíy-i-Zanjání: Surnamed Ḥujjat. "One of the ablest and most formidable champions of the Faith" (*God Passes By,* p. 44), the leader of the Bábís in what Lord Curzon called "the terrific siege and slaughter" they suffered at Zanján where he with 1800 fellow disciples was martyred.

Mullá Ni'matu'lláh-i-Mázindarání: A Bábí martyred at S͟haykh Ṭabarsí.

Mullá Yúsuf-i-Ardibílí: A "Letter of the Living," martyred at S͟haykh Ṭabarsí.

Mustag͟hát͟h: Literally, "He who is invoked." Referring to the appearance of Bahá'u'lláh at the time announced by the Báb.

Naḍr-Ibn-i-Hárit͟h: An opponent of Muḥammad.

Nebuchadnezzar: King of Babylon. In 599 B.C. he captured Jerusalem, and in 588 B.C. he destroyed the city and removed most of the inhabitants to Chaldaea.

Nimrod: In Muḥammadan commentaries represented as the persecutor of Abraham.

Noah: A prophet to whom Muḥammadans give the title of the "Prophet of God," see Gen. 6:10 and Qur'án, súrihs 11, 71, for an account of his life and of the Flood.

Nudbih, Prayer of: A "Lamentation" of the Imám 'Alí.

GLOSSARY AND NOTES

Paradise: A heavenly garden; a state of bliss. The Manifestation is "The Nightingale of Paradise"; His Revelation, "the rustling of the leaves of Paradise"; "the love of God" is itself Paradise.

Párán: Párán is a mountain range north of Sinai and south of Seir; all are sacred as places of revelation. Teman lies in northwest Edam, not far from Párán. See Habakuk 3:3. Moses himself uses "Párán" with special reference to Muḥammad and "Seir" to Jesus Christ: "And he said, The Lord came from Sinai, and rose up from Seir unto them; he shined forth from mount Párán, and he came with ten thousands of saints: from His right hand went a fiery law for them." (Deut. 33:2). Here Moses foretells the coming of three revelations and three prophets after himself, the last being Bahá'u'lláh. Ishmael (Gen. 21:21) founded the Arabian peoples in Párán.

Pentateuch: Literally, "the fivefold volume," referring to the first five books of the Bible.

Pharaoh: The common title of the kings of Egypt. The Pharaoh of the oppression is usually held to be Ramesis II (about 1340 B.C.), and his son and successor Merenptah, the Pharaoh of the Exodus, but this is highly uncertain and the birth of Moses is dated as early as 1520 B.C.

Philosopher's Stone: An imaginary substance which the alchemists formerly sought as a means of converting baser metals into gold.

Phoenix: A bird fabled to exist single, to be consumed by fire by its own act, and to rise again from its ashes.

Primal Will: "The first thing which emanated from God is that universal reality . . . which the people of Bahá call the 'First Will.'" (*Some Answered Questions*, p. 237)

Qá'im: The promised one of Islám.

[266]

GLOSSARY AND NOTES

Qayyúmu'l-Asmá: A commentary on the Súrih of Joseph in the Qur'án, written by the Báb in 1844, and regarded by the Bábís as in effect their Qur'án. (For an outline of its contents, see *God Passes By*, p. 23).

Qiblih: The direction in which the face must be turned in prayer. Qur'án, súrih 2:136–145, establishes Mecca as the Qiblih for Muslims.

Quintessence: An imagined fifth "essence of heaven" in addition to the four elements of earth: hence, the last or highest essence of anything.

Qur'án: The Qur'án (Arabic, "reading"), the holy scriptures of the Muḥammadan faith, revealed by Muḥammad. The verses are built up into chapters called súrihs. It contains 77,974 words and is slightly longer than the New Testament; it was composed over a period of 21 years. The whole book was not arranged until after the Prophet's death, but He is believed to have Himself divided the súrihs and given most of them their present titles. Translation into English by G. Sale (1734) is the most authoritative, but that by J. M. Rodwell (Everyman's Series) is recommended as the best. See also A. J. Arberry, *The Koran Interpreted.*

Rayy: An ancient city near which Ṭihrán was built.

Riḍván: The name of the custodian of Paradise. Bahá'u'lláh uses it to denote Paradise itself.

Rik'ats: Prostrations.

Rúz-bih: A Persian who embraced Christianity and being told a Prophet was about to arise in Arabia journeyed thither and meeting Muḥammad at Koba in His flight to Medina recognized His station and became a Muslim.

Ṣádiq: The sixth of the S͟hí'ih Imáms.

Sadratu'l Muntahá: The name of a tree planted by the Arabs in ancient times at the end of a road, to serve as a guide. As a symbol it denotes the Manifestation of God in His Day.

Sadrih: Literally, Branch.

Ṣáliḥ: An ancient prophet to the Arabs, mentioned in the Qur'án, súrih 7:71–77. Some commentators identify him with the Ṣáliḥ of Genesis 11:13.

Salsabíl: Literally, softly flowing. A fountain of Paradise.

Sámirí: A magician employed by Pharaoh as a rival to Moses. According to Muslims, it was he, not Aaron, who made the golden calf.

"Seal of the Prophets": One of the titles of Muḥammad.

Shaykh Aḥmad: The first of the two forerunners of the Báb, born A.D. 1753, founder of the Shaykhí School and author of 96 books. Died 1831.

Sheba: A town in southern Arabia, referred to in Genesis 10:28; I Kings 10; II Chronicles 9. Symbolically it stands for a dwelling place, a home.

Shí'ih: The problem of succession divides Islám generally into two schools of opinion. According to one view, represented chiefly by the Shí'ihs, the regency is a spiritual matter determined by the Prophet and by those who so succeed Him. According to the other view, that of the Sunnites, the succession goes by popular choice. The Caliph of the Sunnites is the outward and visible Defender of the Faith. The Shí'ih Imám is divinely ordained and gifted with more than human wisdom and authority.

Shoeb: Priest of Midian (Exodus 2:16–21). Moses married his daughter; Exodus 18 gives his name as Jethro.

Shíráz: The capital of the Province of Fárs in Persia; the place of the Báb's birth and the scene of His Declaration in 1844.

Sinai: The mountain where God gave the Law to Moses (Qur'án, súrih 7:139 and Exodus 19).

GLOSSARY AND NOTES

Ṣiráṭ: Literally, bridge or support; denotes the religion of God.

Siyyid Ḥusayn-i-Turshízí: A mujtahid, one of the Seven Martyrs of Ṭihrán.

Siyyid Káẓim: Chief disciple of Shaykh Aḥmad and his successor. Ḥusayn and other distinguished Bábís were among his students. Died December 31, 1843.

Siyyid Yaḥyá, surnamed Vaḥíd: A distinguished divine of great learning who became a Bábí and was martyred after the siege of Nayríz on June 29, 1850, ten days before the death of the Báb.

Súfís: An order of Muḥammadan mystics.

Súrih: A row or course, as of bricks in a wall. A term used exclusively for the chapters of the Qur'án of which there are one hundred and fourteen.

Tablet: A term for a sacred epistle containing a revelation. The giving of the Law to Moses on tables or tablets is mentioned in the Qur'án, súrih 7:142: "We wrote for him (Moses) upon tables (alwah, pl. of lauh) a monition concerning every matter."

Taff (land of): The plain of Karbilá in which vicinity Imám Ḥusayn was martyred.

Thamúd: A tribe of an ancient Hamitic people, inhabiting the borders of Edom and living in caves. They were nearly exterminated by Chedorlaomer, the Elomite conqueror. The survivors fled to Mt. Seir where they dwelt in the time of Isaac and Jacob.

Traditions: The authoritative record of inspired sayings and acts of the Prophet, in addition to the revelation contained in the Qur'án.

'Urvatu'l-Vuthqá: Literally, "the strongest handle," meaning the Faith of God.

GLOSSARY AND NOTES

Yaḥyá: John, the forerunner of Jesus Christ. He was beheaded by Herod.

Yanbú': A compilation of Shí'ih traditions.

Yathrib: The ancient name of the city which was changed to Medinat un-Nabi, the City of the Prophet, or shortly Medina, the city *par excellence*.

Year Sixty: Meaning 1260 A.H., A.D. 1844, the year of the Báb's Declaration.

Zaqqúm: A tree in the Infernal Regions

Zíyárat: Visiting Tablet revealed by the Imám 'Alí.

INDEX

[271]

INDEX

Fasting, 39

Fáṭimih, Tablet of. *See* Tablet of Fáṭimih

Gabriel, 109

God: attaining Presence of, 141–43, 169–70; binding power of Word of, 112; division caused by Word of, 111–12; Essence of, is unknowable, 3, 98–99; known through Manifestations, 99–100, 103–04; names and attributes of, evidenced by all things, 100–02; tests men's faith, 55–57, 58; trust in, 3, 192

Gold: transmutation of copper into, 157

Gospel: contains prophecies of future Manifestation, 22, 24–25, 27; misunderstood by Christian divines, 26, 213; as Word of God, 199

Hamzih, 121

Heaven: symbolic meaning of, 44, 62, 66–68, 71

Húd, 9; Súrih of, 5

Ḥusayn, 126, 167; martyrdom and sainthood of, 128–29; as "Prince of Martyrs," 225

Ibn-i-Ṣúríyá, 84–86

Imám 'Alí, 166; as Commander of Faithful, 119, 164; saying of, on heaven, hell, judgment, and resurrection, 119

'Imrán, 53

Islám: trials of early days of, 217–18

Israel: reason for chastisement of, 18–19, 137–38, 139. *See also* Jews

Jábir: tradition of, 245

Jesus: Cause of, confirmed in Qur'án, 20–21; Christian misinterpretation of prophecies of, 26–28; explanation of prophecies of, 29, 33; forerunner of, 64, 66; gives signs heralding His return, 24–25; and Law of Qiblih, 51; opposition of Israel to, 18; power and sovereignty of, 133–34; prophesies His return, 20, 21, 22; questioned before Pilate and Caiaphas, 132–33; riches concealed in abasement of, 130–31; strengthened with Holy Spirit, 176–77

Jews: belief of, that Hand of God chained up, 136; opposition of, to Jesus, 18; opposition of, to Muḥammad, 135–38. *See also* Israel

John the Baptist: as forerunner of Jesus, 64–65

Joseph, 212, 254

Judgment: Day of, 111, 114, 116

Kafí, 245, 246

Karim, 190

Karím Khán, 184

Knowledge: acme of, 146; as divine bestowal, 46, 184; human and divine, 145–46; as most grievous of veils, 187–88, 214; as one point, 184; revealed in Qur'án, 147; seventy meanings of, 255; trumpet blast of, 196; twenty-seven letters of, 243–44; two kinds of, 46, 69

Lám, 202

Life: true, 114, 120–21

Magi: search of, for Jesus, 64

Man: can potentially reveal all attributes of God, 101; highest grace bestowed on, 138

INDEX

INDEX